TRANSACTIONS OF THE

AMERICAN PHILOSOPHICAL SOCIETY

HELD AT PHILADELPHIA

FOR PROMOTING USEFUL KNOWLEDGE

VOLUME 70, PART 3 · 1980

Isidore of Seville on the Pagan Gods
(*Origines* VIII.11)

KATHERINE NELL MACFARLANE

ASSISTANT PROFESSOR OF CLASSICS, OHIO STATE UNIVERSITY

THE AMERICAN PHILOSOPHICAL SOCIETY

INDEPENDENCE SQUARE: PHILADELPHIA

June, 1980

Library of Congress Catalog
Card Number 79-54274
International Standard Book Number 0-87169-703-3
US ISSN 0065-9746

ISIDORE OF SEVILLE AND THE PAGAN GODS
(ORIGINES VIII.11)

KATHERINE NELL MACFARLANE

CONTENTS

INTRODUCTION

1. ISIDORE'S LIFE.[1]

At the time of Isidore's birth, *ca* A.D. 560, Spain was experiencing the end of a period of turmoil. The country was being unified under the Visigothic kings of Toledo, and in 578 King Reccared would resolve the religious conflict between the Catholic Hispano-Romans and the Arian Visigoths by embracing the Catholic faith.

Isidore's family suffered to some extent from the unsettled nature of the times. His father Severianus was a prominent Hispano-Roman citizen of Cartagena, where Isidore's older brother Leander was born and grew to manhood; but Severianus removed his family to Seville around the time of Isidore's birth, perhaps to escape the invasion of southern Spain by the troops of Justinian.

Isidore was the youngest of the four children of Severianus. He had two brothers, Leander and Fulgentius, and a sister, Florentina. All that is known of Isidore's early years is that his parents died when he was quite young, and that he and Fulgentius and Florentina were raised by Leander, who was some twenty years older than Isidore and already a monk when the family moved to Seville.

[1] The information on Isidore's life and education is taken largely from Jacques Fontaine, *Isidore de Séville et la Culture Classique dans l'Espagne Wisigothique* (Paris: Etudes Augustiniennes, 1959), pp. 5–9, supplemented by Ernest Brehaut, *An Encyclopedist of the Middle Ages: Isidore of Seville* ("Studies in History, Economics and Public Law," **XLVIII**, No. 1 (New York: Columbia University, 1912): pp. 20–22, and William D. Sharpe, *Isidore of Seville: The Medical Writings* (*Transactions of the American Philosophical Society*, New Series **LIV**, Part 2; Philadelphia: The American Philosophical Society, 1964), pp. 6–7.

Leander was later to become the bishop of Seville and the foremost religious leader of Spain. Under the influence of such a brother, it is hardly surprising that all the younger children eventually entered the church: Fulgentius became the bishop of Astigi; Florentina became a nun; and Isidore, after Leander's death in 599, succeeded him to the episcopal see of Seville.

The remainder of his life was uneventful, devoted to religious duties and scholarship. Spain was enjoying an interval of peace and a minor renaissance, and Isidore contributed to the cultural growth of his time. He was highly respected both for his eloquence and for his learning, and he enjoyed the personal friendship of King Sisebut, himself a man of considerable erudition. Two years before his death he presided over the fourth Council of Toledo, and was effective in improving the educational standards of the Spanish clergy. He died at Seville on April 4, 636.

2. ISIDORE'S EDUCATION

It was Isidore's misfortune that his father died before he could have much influence on the boy's education. The elegant prose of Leander's two extant works indicates that Severianus took great pains educating his oldest son, and he would no doubt have done the same for Fulgentius and Isidore. As it happened, the boys were probably enrolled in a monastery school where the curriculum was of an ecclesiastical nature, and much inferior in scope to that which Leander had followed. Beyond this they received a certain amount of schooling from Leander himself, who took a direct hand in their education; it is probably to his brother that Isidore owed his exposure to a variety of authors outside the regular curriculum. At the same time, Leander cannot have had the time or resources to train his brothers in the finer points of rhetoric and literary criticism; in fact, he may not have seen the need of it.

Isidore appears to have emerged from his schooling with a great enthusiasm for learning and a considerable tolerance for pagan culture. Clearly, he was a voracious reader of both pagan and Christian authors and delved into a variety of subjects not usually of interest to churchmen of his age. Unfortunately, he was not trained in the intellectual discipline that ideally should accompany this exuberance. He was lacking in critical acumen, and had an altogether medieval trust in the authority of the written word. Confronted with two contradictory statements, he would dutifully record both, without any attempt to judge between them. He copied down nonsense that even the most perfunctory empirical observation would have shown to be false, and it seems never to have occurred to him that sometimes an author might not intend his words to be taken seriously; at one point (*Origines* xvi.20.4), he unquestioningly records Trimalchio's recipe for Corinthian bronze.

His literary style, though lucid, is pedestrian. In fact, in the majority of his works, including the *Origines*, he contributes little more than the mortar which connects excerpts from other authors, as if he was aware of his deficiencies and had more confidence in the *stilus maiorum* than in his own. Even in works that are entirely his own, there is a labored terseness that compares badly with his brother's command of the Latin language.

3. THE WRITING OF THE *ORIGINES*

Isidore wrote on a wide variety of subjects both sacred and secular in the course of his long life, but his most famous work is his great encyclopedia called the *Origines* or *Etymologiae*. He began this vast compilation at the request of his friend and protégé Braulio, bishop of Saragossa. It must have been the work of many years, taken up as his ecclesiastical duties allowed and interrupted toward the end of his life by failing health. He left the work unfinished, or at least unrevised, at his death and entrusted it to Braulio *ad emendandum*. It was Braulio who divided it arbitrarily into the present twenty books; Isidore had broken down the material only by subject.

4. ISIDORE AND THE ENCYCLOPEDIC TRADITION

The idea of a comprehensive encyclopedia of this sort was not original with Isidore. Since the days of the Roman Republic, scholars had been compiling handbooks and compendia on a variety of topics in an effort to systematize the mass of scholarly information that they had inherited from the Hellenistic world. The first of the great Roman encyclopedic writers was Varro (116–27 B.C.), whose *Disciplinae*, covering the seven liberal arts (plus medicine and architecture), laid the foundation for the *trivium* and *quadrivium;* he also wrote extensively on Roman antiquities and the Latin language. Unfortunately, the only one of his many works to survive, and that only in part, is *De lingua latina*. At about the same time, Verrius Flaccus produced the first lexicon of the Latin language. The following century saw the *Artes* of Celsus and the *Naturalis Historia* of the elder Pliny, and in the reign of Hadrian, Suetonius brought out his *Prata*, a mis-

cellany of information on many topics. As the impulse toward literary creation began to falter in the later Empire, the tendency toward epitome and compilation became more pronounced, and the digest became one of the characteristic genres of the period. Later authors abridged and extracted from earlier ones, to the very great detriment of the general fund of knowledge, which was further depleted by the efforts of the Christian fathers to bring secular learning into line with Christian values. Isidore merely continued a process that had been going on for seven hundred years.

The one innovation which Isidore contributed to this encyclopedic tradition reflected the ambiguous attitude of earlier patristic writers toward pagan learning. Whereas earlier encyclopedists professed only to have gathered together, to a greater or lesser degree, whatever was known about a given topic, Isidore was the first to compile a comprehensive reference work containing, in the words of Braulio, *quaecunque fere sciri debentur*, "practically everything that it is necessary to know."[2] All secular knowledge that was of use to the Christian scholar had been winnowed out and contained in one handy volume; the scholar need search no further.

5. ISIDORE AND THE ANCIENT ETYMOLOGISTS

The ancient study of etymology goes back, like most ancient studies, to the Greeks; but the Roman grammarians, and in particular Varro, devoted considerable attention to it, so that the author of the *Origines* had a rich fund of material upon which to draw. The originality of Isidore's approach to the subject lies in the importance which he attached to it. What to the Roman student of language had been a useful tool for the rhetorician in determining the exact meaning and correct usage of words became for Isidore a fundamental means to all knowledge.[3] Plato debated in the *Cratylus* whether the name of a particular thing is determined by its nature or assigned to it by arbitrary convention. Later etymologists inclined toward the former theory, which Isidore inherited and expanded into the belief that if one could trace the original and uncorrupted sense of a word, one was in a position to understand the essential nature of that which the word represented:

Etymologia est origo vocabulorum, cum vis verbi vel nominis per interpretationem colligitur. . . . Cuius cognitio saepe usum necessarium habet in interpretatione sua. Nam dum videris unde ortum est nomen, citius vim eius intellegis. Omnis enim rei inspectio etymologia cognita planior est.

(*Origines* i.29.1–2)

---

[2] *Elogium* to Isidore attached to Isidore's *De Viris Illustribus*.
[3] Fontaine, p. 41.

Although Isidore goes on to observe that the ancients did not always assign names *secundum naturam*, but sometimes *secundum placitum*, he clearly believed that an etymology of the former sort could be found for almost every word, and sometimes more than one. Varro and those who drew upon him often give multiple derivations for a word, but they generally present them as alternative choices; let the reader determine for himself which one seems the most reasonable. Isidore sees no reason why a word cannot have more than one derivation, each revealing a different aspect of its nature:

Ab actibus autem vocantur, ut Mercurius, quod mercibus praeest; . . .

Mercurium sermonem interpretantur. Nam ideo Mercurius quasi medius currens dicitur appellatus, quod sermo currat inter homines medius.
(*Origines* viii.11.3, 45)

Diabolus Hebraice dicitur deorsum fluens, . . . Graece vero diabolus criminator vocatur, . . .
(*Origines* viii.11.18)

Nymphas deas aquarum putant, dictas a nubibus. . . .
Nymphas deas aquarum, quasi numina lympharum.
(*Origines* viii.11.96)

Isidore has been much ridiculed for the silliness of many of his etymologies, quite unfairly, for he took all or almost all of them from earlier grammarians; among them the most esteemed scholars of the Roman world. Ancient etymology, though not without system, was based upon the superficial resemblances between words rather than an understanding of their historical relationships, and the etymologists, who regarded the possession by two words of a common syllable, or even a common letter, as significant, approached the problem with something of the spirit of the learned nineteenth-century Englishman who observed that "an explanation of British place-names could usually be found in some language if only one had a sufficiency of dictionaries."[4] Some of the more astute ancients remarked on the unsatisfactory nature of such derivations:

Iam sit et "classis" a calando et "lepus levipes" et "vulpes volipes": etiamne a contrariis aliqua sinemus trahi, ut "lucus" quia umbra opacus parum luceat, et "ludus" quia sit longissime a lusu, et "Ditis" quia minime dives? etiamne "hominem" appellari, quia sit humo natus, quasi vero non omnibus animalibus eadem origo, aut illi primi mortales ante nomen inposuerint terrae quam sibi, et "verba" ab aëre verberato? Pergamus: sic perveniemus eo usque, ut "stella" luminis stilla credatur, cuius etymologiae auctorem clarum sane in litteris nominare in ea parte qua a me reprenditur, inhumanum est. Qui vero talia libris complexi sunt, nomina sua ipsi inscripserunt, ingenioseque visus est Gavius "caelibes" dicere veluti "caelites," quod onere gravissimo vacent, idque

Graeco argumento iuvat: ἠΐθεους enim eadem de causa dici adfirmat. nec ei cedit Modestus inventione: nam, quia Caelo Saturnus genitalia absciderit, hoc nomine appellatos, qui uxore careant, ait; Aelius "pituitam," quia petat vitam. Sed cui non post Varronem sit venia? qui "agrum" quia in eo agatur aliquid, et "gragulos" quia gregatim volent, dictos Ciceroni persuadere voluit (ad eum enim scribit), cum alterum ex Graeco sit manifestum dici, alterum ex vocibus avium. Sed hoc tanti fuit vertere, ut "merula" quod sola volat, quasi mera volans nominaretur. quidam non dubitarunt etymologiae subicere omnem nominis causam, ut ex habitu, quem ad modum dixi, "Longos" et "Rufos," ex sono "stertere," "murmurare," etiam derivata, ut a "velocitate" dicitur "velox," et composita pluraque his similia, quae sine dubio aliunde origine dicunt sed arte non egent cuius in hoc opere non est usus nisi in dubiis.
(Quintilian, *Inst. or.* i.6.33–38)

Quintilian's ridicule is leveled particularly at derivations made by the principle called *compositio*, or "etymology by contraction," according to which:

. . . each word is derived from two or more component words, no distinction being drawn between stem and inflectional endings: the only rule is that the first part of the first component, the last part of the last, and at least one letter of the middle components must be represented in the word under analysis.[5]

Examples are Varro's *cura quod cor urat* and the fanciful medieval *cadaver* from *caro data vermibus*. The *Origines* contains numerous examples of *compositio*; from Chapter viii.11 alone consider *Saturnus . . . quod saturetur annis* (§30), *Neptunum quasi nube tonans* (§38), *Mercurius quasi medius currens* (§45), and *Minerva . . . quasi munus artium variarum* (§71).

Quintilian also gives examples of another sort of etymology popular in antiquity, the so-called derivation κατ' ἀντίφρασιν or *ex contrariis*. The principle itself, that the meaning of a word can be traced to its semantic opposite, is sound enough as long as it is applied to euphemisms; Isidore, following Servius, correctly observes that the Manes were so-called because they were *terribiles et inmanes* (*Origines* viii.11.100). But applied to noneuphemistic terms, derivation κατ' ἀντίφρασιν leads to such absurdities as the often cited *lucus a non lucendo* and the example offered by Quintilian, *"ludus" quia sit longissime a lusu*.

Although common sense did occasionally lead the etymologists of antiquity to a correct derivation (Varro, for example, notes that *agrarius* is derived from *ager*), the principles which they followed were such that they were right by accident far more than by design and wrong more often than right. The impression that Isidore is more incompetent than his predecessors is due to the fact that he compiled a vast collection of their assorted *errata*, which he himself was scarcely in a position to correct.

[4] K. M. Elizabeth Murray, *Caught in the Web of Words: James Murray and the Oxford English Dictionary* (New Haven and London: Yale University Press, 1977), p. 53. The languages under consideration included "Persian, American Indian, and Arabic."

[5] W. S. Allen, "Ancient Ideas on the Origin and Development of Language," *Trans. Philolog. Soc.* (1948), p. 54.

6. ISIDORE'S METHODS

Because many of the sources from which Isidore extracted his material for the *Origines* have been lost, it is difficult for the modern commentator to determine how much of the work is borrowed directly or indirectly from earlier authors, and to what degree it bears the stamp of Isidore's own originality. Granted, the latter was never great. Yet a comparison of the sources which have survived with the corresponding passages of the *Origines* often reveals alterations which, if they are not unintentional, indicate a certain creative impulse on the part of the author.

Perhaps a consideration of what we know of Isidore's methods of research and composition will be useful in determining the degree of liberty that he took with his sources. In the dedication of the *Origines* to King Sisebut, Isidore describes the means by which he compiled his encyclopedia:

En tibi, sicut pollicitus sum, misi opus de origine quarundam rerum ex veteris lectionis recordatione collectum atque ita in quibusdam locis adnotatum, sicut extat conscriptum stilo maiorum.

(*Epistolae* VI)

From this, it would appear that his two principal sources of information were memory and *adnotatio*, that is notes which he had copied out in the course of his reading.[6]

It appears from Isidore's statement that he relied more heavily on memory than on written notes, which is unlikely. Fontaine speculates that Isidore, who was a friend and admirer of Sisebut, exaggerated the role of his own personal culture "pour faire valoir aux yeux du prince l'oeuvre qui lui était ainsi offerte."[7] To be sure, the "mnemonic library" had played a substantial role in ancient scholarship, because the nature of the *volumen* made it inconvenient to take notes (both of the reader's hands being required to keep the roll open), or to check references. Because the educational methods of antiquity tended to be conservative, mnemonic training probably figured to some degree in Isidore's schooling. But by his day, the codex had replaced the *volumen* in general use, and it is reasonable to assume, especially considering the verbatim nature of many of his excerpts, that Isidore availed himself of this convenient format both for copious note-taking and for direct reference.

It is most convenient to explain inexact or erroneous quotations in the text of the *Origines* by attributing them to Isidore's faulty memory. But while misrecollection may be to blame in some cases, it is also probable that Isidore, like Homer, nodded, and that many of these discrepancies are the fault of careless notetaking (perhaps, e.g., the substitution of *luto* for *ludo* in *Origines* viii.11.7), or even of deliberate but ill-considered deviations from the source. In the former case, one should bear in mind that the manuscripts that Isidore had to work from were not always of good quality. Fontaine speculates that Isidore may even have relied for a certain amount of his research on the clerks of his *scriptorium*, whose literacy may not have been equal to their task.[8]

We conclude, then, that although Isidore probably depended to some degree on memory, the greater part of the contents of the *Origines* must have been compiled from *adnotationes*—a sort of card file of notes (although in Isidore's case it probably took the form of notebooks) copied down in the course of his readings. Isidore describes the process in the *praefatio* to his *De natura rerum:*

Quae omnia, secundum quod a veteribus viris, ac maxime sicut in litteris catholicorum virorum scripta sunt, proferentes, brevi tabella notavimus.

The question of whether he prepared his works from a general collection of excerpts or researched each of them individually is rather a pointless one. In most instances he probably employed both methods, supplementing reading on specific topics with notes that he had at hand. In the case of the *Origines* he almost certainly reused notes saved from the writing of earlier works; passages identical or almost identical to those in *De natura rerum* and other earlier writings, some containing phrases in Greek, appear in the *Origines*.

The notes, as Isidore himself says, were often abbreviated. There is a tendency among note-takers to jot down only the essential material. This "telegraphic" style is carried over to the text of the *Origines* (*cf.* viii.11.9) and partially explains the concise style of the encyclopedia.

Isidore's method of composition was largely what is known as *conflatio*, the assembling of extracts on a given topic, ideally in a reasonably logical order; although often the passages, including contradictory ones from different authors, will be jumbled together under one broad general heading. Occasionally, as the organization of a section seems to require it, selections will be dovetailed in more complex ways (see for example *Origines* viii.11.43, where a passage of Eusebius is incorporated into one of

---

[6] To these two methods, Fontaine, p. 772, adds a third: direct quotation of extended passages so long and complex that Isidore could not rely on memory (or even, in some cases, understanding) and found direct copying from the source more profitable than making a set of notes. This usually occurs only in chapters dealing with complicated technical subjects; no such passages, I believe, are to be found in *Origines* viii.11.

For this entire section, I have drawn extensively on Fontaine's excellent and detailed analysis of Isidore's working methods.

[7] Fontaine, p. 771.

[8] Fontaine, p. 782.

Augustine, and viii.11.73, where Isidore has intricately combined two passages from Servius).

It is possible that in some instances the combination of primary sources was the work not of Isidore but of some intermediate text now lost to us. Although one should bear in mind that this is a possibility, efforts to distinguish between Isidore's own composition and that of such "composite" intermediaries must usually be futile.

It is often possible to distinguish certain categories of what Dressel calls *verba Isidoriana:*[9] personal additions and adjustments that Isidore himself has made to the extracts from his sources. The first and most obvious of these comes under the heading of "mortar": Isidore had to make certain adjustments in the extracts he used to make them fit together coherently. In *Origines* viii.11, this is particularly the case when he must adapt a passage from one of the patristic writers to his own purposes; *cf.* the drastic alterations which he makes in Lactantius, *Inst. div.* ii.10.12 and ii.10.15 at §8. Fontaine suggests that he also made a number of gratuitous changes in wording in the extracts in order to disguise his sources and make the work more cohesively his own:

C'est le moment, redoutable au chercheur de sources, où l'écrivain défigure souvent ses extraits pour donner au lecteur l'illusion d'une création nouvelle et originale. La synthèse personnelle, amenuisée par la superstition croissante des *auctores*, par le poids écrasant d'une technique millénaire et le souci de transmettre scrupuleusement aux lecteurs la tradition, trouve pourtant dans cette phase son dernier refuge.[10]

These alterations are usually of a minor nature: dropping a prefix or adding one, making insignificant changes in word order, turning an active verb to the passive or replacing a word with its synonym. Related to this is Isidore's persistent practice of attributing a statement not to the author from whom he took it but to the general belief of a large group of people: in *Origines* viii.11, most references to *gentiles, pagani, Hebraei, Graeci, Latini,* and the like are inserted by Isidore. He is probably responsible also for the frequent synonyms and other amplifications slipped in to elucidate details in his sources: *deum hortorum* (viii.11.24), *propter sordes idolatriae* (viii.11.26), and *ac dissidentes* (viii.11.48) are additions of this sort. Finally there may be a number of personal remarks and even attempts at etymologies or symbolic interpretations inspired by those in his sources: The expansion of Servius' *Volcanus* to *Volicanus* and thence to *volans candor* (viii.11.39), the derivation of *Diana* from *Duana, quod luna et die et nocte appareat* (viii.11.56), and the interpretation of Kronos' sickle as a symbol of wisdom *quod intus acuta sit* (viii.11.32), to mention a few. The intermittent moralizing passages in *Origines* viii.11 appear to be expressions of Isidore's own views: *cf.* §§29, 36, and 89. One must always bear in mind, however, that Isidore may have taken all or part of these from sources that are lost; the identification of Isidore's original contributions must remain in all cases tentative.

7. THE SOURCES OF *Origines* VIII.11

The problem of establishing the sources of the *Origines* is complicated both by Isidore's practice of not citing by name the authors from whom he extracts passages (he is so consistent in this regard that Fontaine establishes as a rule of thumb that when an author's name does appear in the text, Isidore is not quoting directly from him[11]) and by his practice of intentionally or unintentionally altering their words. Still, enough passages have been copied out verbatim or nearly so that a number of definite and probable sources can be established.

I have made no attempt to compile a list of sources for the *Origines* as a whole, but only for that portion of it under consideration in this study: *Origines* viii.11. The sources upon which Isidore unquestionably drew for this chapter are as follows:

Augustine: *Contra Faustum Manichaeum; De baptismo contra Donatistas; De civitate Dei; De Genesi ad Litteram; De Trinitate.*

Eusebius (in Jerome's translation and compilation): *Chronici canones.*

Gregory the Great: *Moralia.*

Jerome: *Commentaria in Ecclesiasten; in Epistolam ad Ephesios; in Ezechielem; in Isaiam; in Mattheum; in Prophetas Minores (Osee); De nominibus Hebraicis; De situ et nominibus locorum Hebraicorum; Epistolae, xxii Ad Eustochium; Liber Hebraicarum quaestionum in Genesim.*

Junius Philargyrius: *Explanatio.*

Lactantius: *De ira Dei; Institutiones divinae* (with the *Epitome*).

Prudentius: *Contra Orationem Symmachi.*

Servius: *In Vergilii Carmina Commentarii.*

Solinus: *Collectanea Rerum Memorabilium.*

Tertullian: *Ad nationes; De idololatria; De praescriptione haereticorum.*

Isidore may also have had recourse to Augustine, *De consensu Evangelistarum,* and Cyprian, *Quod idola non dii sunt.*

Servius and Other Scholiasts of Vergil: In the case of Servius, there is a question, not of whether or not Isidore used him—with Augustine's *De civitate Dei* and Lactantius' *Institutiones divinae,* Servius' *Commentarii* constitutes one of the principal sources for

---

[9] E. Dressel, "De Isidori originum fontibus," *Rivista di Filologia e di Istruzione Classica* **3** (1875): pp. 207–268.
[10] Fontaine, p. 769.

[11] Fontaine, p. 745.

Origines viii.11—but of which version of Servius he used. Two versions have come down to us, the shorter which is generally attributed to Servius alone (whether or not he actually wrote it) and the so-called Servius Danielis or Servius *auctus* in which the commentary of Servius is supplemented with extracts from another and better commentary on the works of Vergil (herein designated D), which may be that of Aelius Donatus.[12] Fontaine is of the opinion that the text of Servius *auctus* had already been complied in Isidore's day and that he had access to a copy.[13] The only textual evidence for this (a passage in which Isidore quotes both the text of Servius and the text of D in the proper sequence) that occurs in *Origines* viii.11 is the one in §34 (*et Iuppiter quasi iuvans pater, hoc est, omnibus praestans;* cf. Servius, *unde et Iuppiter dictus, quasi iuvans pater. . . . quod ipse* omnibus *praestare consuevit*), which by itself is hardly conclusive; but Fontaine would have found other examples of this sort elsewhere in the *Origines* to support his statement. In several sections (see §§37, 44, 53, 61, 75, 84, 98, and 99) Isidore does quote extensively from D; so that it can be safely said that Isidore had access to either Servius *auctus* or at least the shorter Servius and a copy of D, which may have been the commentary of Aelius Donatus. It is not unlikely that he had both Servius *auctus* and D.

Related to the question of whether Isidore used Servius *auctus* or took his excerpts directly from D is the problem posed by two passages in *Origines* viii.11 (§§82–83 and 96–97), which occur almost verbatim in the *Explanatio* attributed to Junius Philargyrius on the *Eclogues* of Vergil, only in much paraphrased form or not at all in the shorter Servius, and not at all in the excerpts from D in Servius *auctus*. It is reasonably certain that Isidore took the material in §§96–97 directly from Philargyrius, since he reproduces a mistake that Philargyrius makes, and therefore it is entirely possible that he took that in §§82–83 from the same source. In the case of §§82–83, however, Isidore's wording is sufficiently different from that of Philargyrius to admit of another possibility: Philargyrius probably drew upon Donatus; Isidore may have done likewise, and the passage at *Origines* viii.11.82–83 may have occurred originally in Donatus, whence it was copied by Philargyrius and Isidore, but not by Servius or the compiler of Servius *auctus*.

Finally, *Origines* viii.11 contains evidence of Vergilian scholia based on Servius and intermediary between Servius and Isidore, which have not survived to our day. An instance of this occurs at §100, the curious passage on the Manes, originally

from Servius, *Aen.* iii.63. The information in the section is in quite a different order than the one in which it appears in Servius, which in itself is unusual; Isidore usually copies more or less directly from Servius, and while he may omit portions he seldom tampers with the order. But more significantly, the material in the passage is attributed not to Servius but to Apuleius, which is certainly wrong. It is possible but unlikely that Isidore himself took the excerpt from Servius and later attributed it to Apuleius. There is no indication apart from this passage that he was familiar with Apuleius or used him as a source, and, as has been pointed out, he almost never cites the author of a source from which he has taken material. It follows, then, that Isidore drew for this passage upon an intermediate scholiast who excerpted his material from Servius but attributed it incorrectly to Apuleius. Other passages which may be from this same scholiast (they contain material from Servius but in a different order) are to be found in *Origines* viii.11.49, 65, 73, 76, and 80.

Varro: *Origines* viii.11 contains a great deal of material from Varro's *Antiquities* which Isidore took from Augustine's *De civitate Dei*. Whether or not Isidore also had direct access to some or all of the works of Varro remains an unanswerable question. Fontaine says that he did not,[14] and I have found no instance in which he quotes a surviving text of Varro closely enough and at sufficient length to justify arguing to the contrary. On the other hand, there are a number of etymologies in *Origines* viii.11 that correspond rather closely to ones in the surviving portions of *De lingua latina* (compare §§30/*L.L.* v.64; 50/*L.L.* v.73; 57/*L.L.* v.69; 87/*L.L.* vii.36) and have no other identifiable source. Moreover Arnobius, whom Isidore almost certainly did not use as a source for *Origines* viii.11, observes (*Adv. nat.* iii.40):

Varro, qui sunt introrsus, atque in intimis penetralibus coeli deos esse censet quos loquimur, nec eorum numerum nec nomina sciri.

Isidore, at *Origines* viii.11.99, has

Penates gentiles dicebant omnes deos quos domi colebant. Et penates dicti quod essent in penetralibus, id est in secretis. Hi dei quomodo vocebantur, vel quae nomina habuerint, ignoratur.

The passage in Isidore is sufficiently different from that of Varro that a case cannot be made for direct borrowing, but it is possible that Isidore did make use of one or more abridgements of Varro, on the same order as Festus' abridgement of the lexicon of Verrius Flaccus.

Eucherius: Eucherius, a fifth-century bishop of Lyon, composed a short work called the *Instructiones* in two books, the second of which was taken almost

[12] For a convincing argument in favor of this view, see E. K. Rand, "Is Donatus' Commentary on Virgil Lost?" *Classical Quarterly* 10 (1916): pp. 158–164.
[13] Fontaine, p. 749.

[14] Fontaine, p. 749.

entirely from works of Jerome and gave the Latin equivalents of names found in the Bible. It seems unlikely that Isidore would have known of Eucherius, yet several passages in the first twenty-eight sections of *Origines* viii.11 echo his chapter in the *Instructiones* "De idolis" more closely than they do the corresponding passages in Jerome (see §§18, 19, 23, 24, and 26 in the commentary). For example, in §19, Isidore has *Satanas in Latino sonat adversarius sive transgressor*. Jerome (*Interp. Hebr. nom.* De Luca S) has *Satanas adversarius sive transgressor*, but Eucherius supplies the verb used by Isidore and also the reference to Latin: *Satana in Latinum sonat adversarius sive transgressor*. This is not to say that Isidore used Eucherius in place of Jerome; if he used him at all it was in conjunction with other authors that Eucherius himself had used as sources (cf. §23, where he has apparently begun from Eucherius and used Eucherius' sources Jerome and Servius to supplement the passage).

The Pagan Poets: There is no decisive evidence in *Origines* viii.11 that Isidore referred directly to the pagan poets Vergil, Ovid, and Horace as he was writing. He often does quote passages from them, but either cites their names, so that it is probable that he took the quotations from intermediate sources (many of which can be identified: Lactantius, §68; Lactantius or Augustine, §70), or in the rare instance when he does not (cf. §78), takes the quotation from an identifiable intermediate source that also does not. However, it may be noted that the passage in §52, *Mars autem apud Thracos Gradivus*, seems to indicate that Isidore referred back ˌto Vergil to tie together two pieces of information in Servius. Servius gives the identity of Mars Gradivus and notes that Getici are Thracians, but does not supply the connection between the two, which is to be found in the *Aeneid*, iii.35: *Gradivumque patrem, Geticis qui praesidet arvis.*

8. ISIDORE'S USE OF HIS SOURCES: DIFFERENCES IN INTENT

Although Isidore compiled his encyclopedia almost entirely from information copied from earlier authors, it was still necessary for him to impose a process of selection on the material available to him. His purposes in writing the *Origines* were not necessarily those of his sources. As its name implies, the *Origines* is primarily concerned with discovering how the subjects under discussion came about, primarily (though not exclusively) as revealed by the etymologies of their names.

In the chapter on the pagan gods (*Origines* viii.11), Isidore is concerned with three sorts of origins:

1. The origin of the worship of the pagan gods, which Isidore explains, following Lactantius, in euhe-

meristic terms, with a nod to demonism:

Quos pagani deos asserunt, homines olim fuisse produntur, et pro uniuscuiusque vita vel meritis coli apud suos post mortem coeperunt, . . . In quorum etiam laudibus accesserunt et poetae, et conpositis carminibus in caelum eos sustulerunt. Nam quorundam et inventiones artium cultu peperisse dicuntur, ut Aesculapio medicina, Vulcano fabrica. Ab actibus autem vocantur ut Mercurius, quod mercibus praeest; Liber a libertate. Fuerunt etiam et quidam viri fortes aut urbium conditores quibus mortuis homines, qui eos dilexerunt, simulacra finxerunt, ut haberent aliquod ex imaginum contemplatione solacium; sed paulatim hunc errorem persuadentibus daemonibus ita in posteris inrepisse, ut quos illi pro sola nominis memoria honoraverunt, successores deos existimarent atque colerent.

(*Origines* viii.11.1–5)

That is, the gods were once men who because of the benefits which they had conferred on their people were honored by them after their death, and worshiped as gods by later generations, who were persuaded to this folly by demons.

2. The etymologies of the names of the gods. What Isidore regarded as the connection between who the gods actually were and the origin of their names is not perfectly clear. In §84, the name of Queen Isis becomes the Egyptian word for "earth." But in §3, Isidore states that some of the gods were given names (presumably by the *posteri* who regarded them as gods) which were related to their sphere of authority (*Ab actibus autem vocatur, ut Mercurius quod mercibus praeest; Liber a libertate*); these would, of course, not be the original names of the deified mortals. At §29, however, he seems to be arguing that the names by which the gods are known were actually those of the original mortals, and that the pagan poets were responsible for contriving false etymologies for them in order to credit these "gods" with powers that they never had.

Quaedam autem nomina deorum suorum gentiles per vanas fabulas ad rationes physicas conantur traducere, eaque in causis elementorum conposita esse interpretantur. Sed hoc a poetis totum fictum est, ut deos suos ornarent aliquibus figuris, quos perditos ac dedecoris infamia plenos fuisse confitentur. Omnino enim fingendi locus vacat, ubi veritas cessat.

Yet these seem to be the etymologies that he recorded for the remainder of *Origines* viii.11. It may be, of course, that he did not even draw the conclusion that because the source of the etymologies (or in some cases of the names themselves), i.e., the pagan poets, was false, the etymologies/names themselves were likewise false. But assuming that he did recognize that these etymologies were false according to his introductory arguments, why did he go on to devote the rest of the chapter to explaining them? The explanation must be that he felt justified in giving the false etymologies of the names of false gods because it enabled him to demonstrate how the pagans in their delusion came to believe that these were gods, and to worship them. The name reveals the nature, they would argue; if the name of a hero, say Neptunus, can be made to indicate that he is an elemental force, then he is actually a god and should be so honored. The process can be seen in §§34–36: Interpret a man's name to mean *iuvans pater*, address him as *Optimus*, and in spite of shameless conduct unworthy of a man, let alone a god, he will come to be regarded as a deity. It should be observed that Isidore takes no responsibility for the etymologies of the names of the pagan gods, but is always interposing *fertur, dictus est,* or something of the sort, which he does not do with the etymologies which he discusses in the first part of the chapter. These he evidently regarded as genuine; they have to do with idolatry, demons, Satan, Antichrist, and certain Middle-Eastern gods whom the pious Hebrews recognized as false and named accordingly.

3. Connected with this is the explanation in symbolic or allegorical terms of certain attributes and activities of the gods: physical characteristics such as the sickle of Saturn (§32), the lameness of Vulcan (§41), Liber's vineleaf crown and horns (§44), Mercury's caduceus (§§47–48), the arrows of Diana (§56) and Cupid (§80), the Gorgon's head on Minerva's aegis (§73); traditional behavior, such as the adultery of Mars (§51); and certain subordinate roles connected with a god's principal area of power; for example Liber, god of lust, is also the god of wine *propter excitandum libidinem* (§43), and Mercury, god of speech, is also the god of commerce *quia inter vendentes et ementes sermo fit medius* and patron of thieves *quia sermo animos audientium fallit* (§§45–47).

Isidore is not interested in myths *per se*, which he regarded as *vanae fabulae* (§29) and *fabulosa figmenta* (§89). He only includes them where they serve to further his own purposes, such myths as support the euhemeristic theory of the origin of the gods. For example, he includes in §35 certain of the amorous adventures of Jupiter, because they show that he was not only a man but *incestus in suis, inpudicus in extraneis* (§34); he explains the myth of the creation of man by Prometheus by saying that he actually invented the art of making statues out of clay (§8). In either case the deeds of ordinary mortals were exaggerated by poets to make them seem those of gods. He also records myths which were thought by the pagans to explain the origin of a practice (in §33, the infant sacrifice of the Carthaginians is traced to the myth of Saturn devouring his children), certain physical phenomena (the story of the laming of Vulcan in §§40–41 is thought to explain why lightning falls through the air and why fire does not rise straight up but staggers back and forth like a lame man), the name of a particular god (the battle of Apollo and Python in §§54–55 is told

to explain why the god is called Pythius; at §75, Athena is said to be named Pallas because she slew a giant of that name), or the nature of a god (the birth of Athena from the head of Jupiter, §72, signifies that reason is to be found *in capite et cerebro*).

As a Christian encyclopedist, Isidore differs in his approach from both his Christian and his pagan sources. The patristic writers upon whom he drew, such as Lactantius and Augustine, were engaged in a struggle to the death with paganism. As a result, the information they incorporated about the pagan gods was the foundation of tightly reasoned arguments ridiculing the gods and demonstrating the many inconsistencies in the pagan religion. Many of the arguments they employed were originally those of pagan philosophers, who accepted conventional paganism no more than the Christians did; for example, Euhemerus developed the theory around 300 B.C. that the gods were no more than deified men. The Christians felt that using pagan arguments against the gods strengthened their own case: even the very people who were supposed to believe such things could see that they were nonsense.

By Isidore's day, the battle between Christianity and paganism had been brought to a decisive conclusion. He can hardly have felt that paganism any longer posed a serious threat to the Christian establishment, and he evinces no great interest in the elaborate refutations of paganism by Augustine and the other patristic writers; he may even have felt privately about them as he did about Cicero's rhetorical works: *ita copiose, ita varie, ut eam lectori admirari in promptu sit, conprehendere inpossibile* (*Origines* ii.2.1). He extracts from them such information as he needs concerning the gods, but only such arguments against them as serve to explain their origin: Euhemerism, and to a small degree demonism. In so doing, as Fontaine points out,[16] he makes no distinction between monuments of Christian thought and the lowliest pagan scholia: both are mines to be worked for the information they contain, with no particular regard for the original intent of their authors.

In fact, at first glance Isidore seems to be closer in spirit to pagan antiquaries like Varro and scholiasts like Servius than to any of the patristic writers. These commentators are full of attempts to rationalize the pagan gods and myths, to explain in symbolic terms their names and attributes—very much the sort of thing that Isidore does in the *Origines*—in an effort to make the old gods and myths acceptable to the sophisticated pagan who could not accept them literally. But Isidore is above all a Christian and he can accept of the rationalized explanations of the gods only those that

---

[16] Fontaine, p. 791.

are compatible with Christian doctrine and do not present the pagan gods in any form as suitable objects for worship. He includes what is incompatible with Christianity—Servius and the extracts from Varro in Augustine's *De civitate Dei* are two of his principal sources for *Origines* viii.11—but he informs the reader first and last that it is all so much empty fabrication and not to be taken seriously.

If Isidore had no need to refute the pagan gods and regarded as *gentilium fabulosa figmenta* the pagan attempts to rationalize them, why should he bother to include a chapter on the pagan gods in his encyclopedia at all? I think the answer is that Isidore, like most of the Christian intellectuals before him, regarded pagan culture with a degree of ambivalence. He was first of all a Christian and could not accept it without reservation, for it contained much that was at variance with the Christian faith. On the other hand, he was aware that there was an element of value in pagan culture that deserved to be studied and transmitted. But one could not read very far in most of the pagan authors (and particularly not in that most edifying poet Vergil) without stumbling across the ubiquitous deities of paganism. And lest the Christian reader be misled as to their true nature, it was better for the author of the definitive encyclopedia of knowledge to make

it clear to the reader that these were only men who at the instigation of demons came to be worshiped and that all other attempts to explain their nature were false, than to leave him to blunder along in ignorance: *et cognoscetis veritatem et veritas liberabit vos*, for the study of classical literature no less than in other respects.

Besides this, however, I suspect that Isidore had his own private reasons for undertaking a study of the pagan gods. Fontaine speaks of "son attachement à la connaissance désintéressée"[16] with respect to ancient literature, and reading through *Origines* viii.11, one is aware of the tension between Isidore's dutiful Christianity, which finds expression in the pious sentiments of §§29, 36, and 89, and his genuine interest in what the pagans had to say about their gods. In fact, if one does not read the chapter through carefully from beginning to end, one is in danger of missing the former altogether. And while this was most certainly not Isidore's intent, such denunciations as appear in §§29, 36, and 89 were very possibly far from his mind as he leafed through his Servius searching out this or that bit of information on the gods of the pagans.

---

[16] Fontaine, p. 809.

ORIGINES VIII.11: DE DIIS GENTIUM

TEXT AND COMMENTARY

1. *Quos pagani deos asserunt, homines olim fuisse produntur, et pro uniuscuiusque vita vel meritis coli apud suos post mortem coeperunt, ut apud Aegyptum Isis, apud Cretam Iovis, apud Mauros Iuba, apud Latinos Faunus, apud Romanos Quirinus.*

This opening statement concerning the euhemeristic origin of the pagan gods appears to be Isidore's own (like vague references to *pagani, Iudaei, gentiles, Graeci,* etc. generally), although the expression *homines fuisse produntur* or a close approximation occurs in several patristic writers (*cf.* Augustine, *De cons. evang.* i.23; *De civ. Dei* iv.27, vi.7, vii.35; Lactantius, *Inst. div.* i.15.1; *De ira Dei* 11). The passages that agree most closely with Isidore's wording are Augustine, *De civ. Dei* viii.5 (*sed ipsi etiam maiorum gentium di, . . . homines fuisse produntur*) and Tertullian, *Ad nat.* ii.12 (*et ideo, qui in ista specie unum tuemur propositum demonstrandi illos omnes homines fuisse); Isidore clearly knew the passage in Tertullian, because he continues to quote from it elsewhere (cf. §30 below). The passage pro uniuscuiusque . . . coeperunt* is from Augustine, *De civ. Dei* vi.8 (*in quibus omnibus aut homines fuisse intelleguntur et pro uniuscuiusque vita vel morte sacra*

eis constituta, . . .). The sentiment is voiced by other authors, both pagan and Christian (Cicero, *De nat. deor.* ii.24.62, iii.19.50; *De leg.* ii.18; Tertullian, *Apol.* 11; Lactantius, *De ira Dei* 11; *Inst. div.* i.15.8). Isidore took his list of examples from this last passage: *. . . summa veneratione coluerunt, ut Aegypti Isidem, Mauri Iubam, Macedones Cabirum, Poeni Uranum, Latini Faunum, Sabini Sancum, Romani Quirinum.* He may have deleted Cabirus, Uranus, and Sancus from his own list because they were altogether unfamiliar to him (he refers to Uranus only as Caelus elsewhere in the text), or perhaps he was quoting the passage either from memory or from his own paraphrase; note that while he reproduces the sense of the passage, he has converted the action from active to passive (*coluerunt* becomes *coli . . . coeperunt*). The insertion of *apud Cretam Iovis* is a more complicated problem. The association of Jupiter with Crete is common enough; perhaps Isidore had in mind Cyprian, *Quod idola dii non sint* 4 or Lactantius, *Inst. div.* i.11.46, 48. But it is unclear why he uses the nominative form *Iovis* instead of *Iuppiter*.

2. *Eodem quoque modo apud Athenas Minerva, apud Samum Iuno, apud Paphos Venus, apud Lemnos Vulcanus, apud Naxos Liber, apud Delos Apollo. In quorum etiam laudibus accesserunt et poetae, et conpositis carminibus in caelum eos sustulerunt.*

The source for the first part of this passage is Lactantius, *Inst. div.* i.15.9 (*eodem utique modo Athenae Minervam, Samos Iunonem, Paphos Venerem, Vulcanum Lemnos, Liberum Naxos, Apollinem Delos*), a continuation of the passage quoted in §1. Isidore has apparently mistaken the Greek nominatives Paphos, Lemnos, Naxos, and Delos for the accusative plurals of the inhabitants of these islands. The reference to the poets is from Lactantius, *Inst. div.* i.15.13 (*accesserunt etiam poetae et compositis ad voluptatem carminibus in caelum eos sustulerunt*).

3. *Nam quorundam et inventiones artium cultu peperisse dicuntur, ut Aesculapio medicina, Vulcano fabrica. Ab actibus autem vocantur, ut Mercurius, quod mercibus praeest; Liber a libertate.*

There appears to be some textual corruption in the sentence *Nam quorundam . . . fabrica,* which is virtually meaningless as it stands in the Lindsay text. The source is Lactantius, *Inst. div.* i.18.21: *artes quoque inventoribus suis inmortalitatem peperisse dicuntur, ut Aesculapio medicina, Volcano fabrica.* Thus *peperisse* appears to be sound, and the problem lies in the confusion of *inventoribus/inventiones* and *artes/artium cultu.* The most obvious emendation is to change *cultu* (as a miscopying of *cultū*) to *cultum.* This is the reading preferred by Arevalo, and it has some manuscript support. It still does not reproduce the sense of Lactantius, but it can be argued that Isidore does often alter or even misunderstand and misquote his sources. (An alternative emendation that does not do such violence to the source would be the insertion of *inmortalitatem* after *inventiones.*) The source of *ab actibus . . . libertate* is Servius, *Aen.* iv.638: *Ab actibus autem vocantur ut Iuppiter iuvans pater, Mercurius quod mercibus praeest, Liber a libertate.* It is odd that Isidore mentions the (probably correct) etymology of *Mercurius* here, yet ignores it in his discussion of Mercury (§§45–48), preferring there Varro's foolish etymology from *medius currens.* He omits the reference to Jupiter in this section, but quotes it in §34 below.

4. *Fuerunt etiam et quidam viri fortes aut urbium conditores, quibus mortuis homines, qui eos dilexerunt, simulacra finxerunt, ut haberent aliquod ex imaginum contemplatione solacium; sed paulatim hunc errorem persuadentibus daemonibus ita in posteris inrepsisse, ut quos illi pro sola nominis memoria honoraverunt, successores deos existimarent atque colerent.*

The immediate source of most of this section appears to be Lactantius, *Inst. div.* i.15.3–4 and 8:

Deinde ipsi reges cum cari fuissent iis, quorum vitam composuerant, magnum sui desiderium mortui reliquerunt. itaque homines eorum simulacra finxerunt, ut haberent aliquod ex imaginum contemplatione solacium, progressique longius per amorem memoriam defunctorum colere coeperunt, ut et gratiam referre bene meritis viderentur et successores eorum adlicerent ad bene imperandi cupiditatem. . . . privatim vero singuli populi gentis aut urbis suae conditores, seu viri fortitudine insignes erant seu feminae castitate mirabiles, summa veneratione coluerunt, . . .

If this is so, Isidore has taken greater liberties in paraphrasing than he usually does. The demons crept in from Augustine, *De civ. Dei* vi.8:

in quibus omnibus aut homines fuisse intelleguntur et pro uniuscuiusque vita vel morte sacra eis sollemnia constituta, hunc errorem insinuantibus firmantibusque daemonibus, aut certe ex qualibet occasione inmundissimi spiritus fallendis humanis mentibus inrepsisse.

Isidore seems to have misread the passage; *hunc errorem* as the object of *insinuantibus firmantibusque daemonibus* and the final *inrepsisse* does explain Isidore's rather puzzling use of indirect discourse, *hunc errorem . . . inrepsisse.* For the sense of the section generally, *cf.* Augustine, *De civ. Dei* vii.35, *Aut ergo daemonum . . . supponebant.*

5. *Simulacrorum usus exortus est, cum ex desiderio mortuorum constituerentur imagines vel effigies, tamquam in caelum receptis, pro quibus se in terris daemones colendi supposuerunt, et sibi sacrificari a deceptis et perditis persuaserunt.*

The source of §5, somewhat rearranged, is Augustine, *Contra Faustum* xxii.17:

maxime cum ex desiderio mortuorum constituerentur imagines, unde simulacrorum usus exortus est; et maiore adulatione divini honores deferrentur tamquam in coelum receptis, pro quibus se in terris daemonia colenda supponerent et sibi sacrificari a deceptis et perditis flagitarent.

6. *Simulacra autem a similitudine nuncupata, eo quod manu artificis ex lapide aliave materia eorum vultus imitantur in quorum honore finguntur. Ergo simulacra vel pro eo quod sunt similia, vel pro eo quod simulata atque conficta; unde et falsa sunt.*

Simulacra . . . nuncupata is from Jerome, *De nom. Hebr.*, De Ezech. S (*Semel idolum. Et notandum quod Latinus sermo sit in hebrais voluminibus a similitudine, unde et simulacra dicuntur*), from which Isidore continues to quote in the following section. The rest of the sentence, *eo quod manu . . . finguntur,* may echo Lactantius, *Inst. div.* ii.2.11–12 (*simulacra . . . quae essent aut incultus et horridus lapis aut materia informis ac rudis, nisi fuissent ab homine formata. homo igitur illorum quasi parens putandus est, per cuius manus nata sunt*), or it may be Isidore's own elaboration. I could find no source for the etymology of *simulacrum* from *similia* (perhaps it is ultimately from Varro); *vel pro eo . . . sunt*, however, is adapted from Lactantius, *Inst. div.* ii.18.2–3: *quod quidem de nomine ipso apparere sapienti potest, quidquid enim simulatur, id falsum sit necesse est.*

7. *Et notandum quod Latinus sermo sit in Hebraeis. Apud eos enim idolum sive simulacrum Semel dicitur. Iudaei dicunt quod Ismael primus simulacrum luto fecerit.*

The equation of simulacrum with Hebrew *semel* (Arevalo's *selem/zelem* is an error) is from Jerome, *De nom. Hebr.*, De Ezech. S, quoted in §6. Note that Isidore has omitted *voluminibus* after *Hebraeis*. Jerome evidently regarded *semel* as a borrowing from Latin, from *simulacrum*, although elsewhere (cf. §18) he sees nothing wrong in deriving the same word from two different etymologies in two different and unrelated languages. Isidore accepts this naïve approach to linguistic theory without question. The reference to Ismael is a particularly interesting mis-reading of Jerome, *Hebr. quaest. in Genes.* 21:9: *Dupliciter itaque hoc ab Hebraeis exponitur: sive quod idola ludo fecerit, . . . sive quod adversum Isaac, quasi maioris aetatis, ioco sibi et ludo primogenita vindicaret. Quod quidem Sara audiens non tulit.* Isidore, influenced no doubt by the passages from Lactantius which he quotes in §8, has written *luto* for *ludo*.

8. *Gentiles autem primum Prometheum simulacrum hominum de luto finxisse perhibent, ab eoque natam esse artem simulacra et statuas fingendi. Unde et poetae ab eo homines primum factos esse confingunt figurate propter effigies.*

This section is from Lactantius, *Inst. div.* ii.10.12

verum quia poetas dixeram non omnino mentiri solere, sed figuris involvere et obscurare quae dicant, non dico esse mentitos, sed primum omnium Promethea simulacrum hominis formasse de molli ac pingui luto ab eoque primo natam esse artem statuas et simulacra fingendi

and ii.10.15 (*de hac hominis fictione poetae quoque quamvis corrupte, tamen non aliter tradiderunt: namque hominem de luto a Prometheo factum esse dixerunt*). Cf. also Augustine, *De civ. Dei* xviii.8.

9. *Apud Graecos autem Cecrops, sub quo primum in arce oliva orta est, et Atheniensium urbs ex Minervae appellatione nomen sortita est.*

10. *Hic primus omnium Iovem appellavit, simulacra repperit, aras statuit, victimas inmolavit, nequaquam istiusmodi rebus in Graecia umquam visis.*

These two sections are taken almost verbatim from the *praefatio* of Jerome's translation of Euse-

bius' *Chronica:*

Porro iste est Cecrops Difyes indigena sub quo primum in arce oliva orta est, et Atheniensium urbs ex Minervae appellatione sortita nomen. Hic primus omnium Iovem appellavit, simulacra repperit, aram statuit, victimas immolavit, nequaquam istius modi rebus in Graecia umquam visis.

Isidore has omitted the unfamiliar epithet *Difyes* (*Diphyes*, "of double form," because Cecrops had a serpent's tail in place of legs), as well as the *indigena* and the verb which in his abbreviated style he leaves understood.

11. *Idolatria idolorum servitus sive cultura interpretatur. Nam* λατρεία *Graece, Latine servitus dicitur, quae quantum ad veram religionem adtinet, nonnisi uni et soli Deo debetur.*

Isidore probably took his quite correct etymology of *idolatria* from a combination of Tertullian, *De idol.* 3 (*Inde idololatria omnis circa omne idolum famulatus et servitus*) and Augustine, *De trin.* ii.6.13 (*necesse est ut huic eam servitutem debeamus, qua nonnisi Deo serviendum est, quae Graece appellatur* λατρεία); cf. also *De civ. Dei* vii.32 (*verum etiam sacra, sacerdotia, . . . et quidquid aliud ad eam servitutem pertinet quae Deo debetur, et Graece proprie* λατρεία *dicitur*).

12. *Hanc sicut inpia superbia sive hominum sive daemonum sibi exhiberi vel iubet vel cupit, ita pia humilitas vel hominum vel angelorum sanctorum sibi oblatam recusat, et cui debetur ostendit.*

I have been unable to discover any source for this passage. It may be Isidore's own effort at moralizing, although the elegance of its style argues against this.

13. *Idolum autem est simulacrum quod humana effigie factum et consecratum est, iuxta vocabuli interpretationem.* Εἶδος *enim Graece formam sonat, et ab eo per diminutionem idolum deductum aeque apud nos formulam facit. Igitur omnis forma vel formula idolum se dici exposcit.*

The ultimate source of *idolum autem est simulacrum* may be, as *TLL* states, Tertullian, *De idol.* 3 (*at ubi artifices statuarum et imaginum et omnis generis simulacrorum diabolus saeculo intulit, rude illud negotium humanae calamitatis et nomen de idolis consecutum est et profectum*). However, Isidore himself seems to have gotten it directly from Eucherius, the fifth-century bishop of Lyons; the second book of his *Instructiones* contains a chapter *De idolis*, with the passage *Idola simulacra, Graecum est*. Since this chapter draws heavily upon Jerome, he may be the ultimate source of this etymology. The remainder of the section, *iuxta vocabuli . . . exposcit*, is taken from Tertullian, *De idol.* 3: *Ad hoc necessaria est vocabuli interpretatio.* Εἶδος *Graece formam sonat; ab eo per diminutionem* εἴδωλον *deductum aeque apud nos formulam fecit. Igitur omnis forma vel formula idolum se dici exposcit.* The Greek εἴδωλον has been transliterated into Latin characters in Isidore; this may be the work of a later copyist.

14. *Inde idolatria omnis circa omnem idolum famulatus et servitus. Quidam vero Latini ignorantes Graece inperite dicunt idolum ex dolo sumpsisse nomen, quod diabolus creaturae cultum divini nominis invexit.*

Inde idolatria . . . servitus is a continuation of Tertullian, *De idol.* 3, which Isidore was quoting in §13: *Inde idololatria omnis circa omne idolum famulatus et servitus.* Lindsay makes no comment in his apparatus on the form *omnem idolum;* since *idolum,* from Greek εἴδωλον, is invariably neuter, it is either a solecism on Isidore's part or an error in the text unemended by the editor (*cf. Epistolae* A, *dum a mihi litteras, karissime fili, suscipis,* which should certainly be emended to *dum amici litteras*). Arevalo's text has simply *circa idolum,* which offers no solution to the problem. What follows may be Isidore's own observation, although he was hardly in a position to deride *Latini ignorantes Graece.* Whom he had in mind it is impossible to say. Cassiodorus gives the etymology from *dolus, Expos. Psalm.* xcvi.7: *Idolum quippe dictum est quod ipsum sit dolum, id est, hominum falsitate repertum.* A passage of Filastrius (*Divers. heres. lib.* cix.7: *Nam et ipsud nomen idoli species doli et famae praevaricatio de interpretatione Greca est nuncupatum*) cleverly incorporates both etymologies.

15. *Daemonas a Graecis dictos aiunt, quasi δαήμονας, id est peritos ac rerum scios. Praesciunt enim futura multa, unde et solent responsa aliqua dare.*

This section is compressed from Lactantius, *Inst. div.* ii.14.6:

daemones autem grammatici dictos aiunt quasi δαήμονας, id est peritos ac rerum scios: hos enim putant deos esse. sciunt illi quidem futura multa, sed non omnia, quippe quibus penitus consilium dei scire non liceat, et ideo solent responsa in ambiguos exitus temperare.

It is odd that Isidore should omit the warning about the ambiguous nature of demonic oracles, but he evidently found the statement that they knew *futura multa* adequate to explain the etymology.

16. *Inest enim illis cognitio rerum plus quam infirmitati humanae, partim subtilioris sensus acumine, partim experientia longissimae vitae, partim per Dei iussum angelica revelatione. Hi corporum aeriorum natura vigent.*

Isidore takes this section, considerably paraphrased, from Augustine, *De Gen. ad Lit.* ii.17.37:

Ideoque fatendum est, quando ab istis vera dicuntur, instinctu quodam occultissimo dici quam nescientes humanae mentes patiuntur. Quod cum ad decipiendos homines fit, spirituum seductorum operatio est: quibus

quaedam vera de temporalibus rebus nosse permittitur, partim quia subtilioris sensus acumine, partim quia corporibus subtilioribus vigent, partim experientia callidiore propter tam magnam longitudinem vitae; partim sanctis Angelis quod ipsi ab omnipotente Deo discunt, etiam jussu eius sibi revelantibus, qui merita humana occultissimae justitiae sinceritate distribuit.

17. *Ante transgressionem quidem caelestia corpora gerebant. Lapsi vero in aeriam qualitatem conversi sunt, nec aeris illius puriora spatia, sed ista caliginosa tenere permissi sunt, qui eis quasi carcer est usque ad tempus iudicii. Hi sunt praevaricatores angeli, quorum Diabolus princeps est.*

The first two sentences of this section, like §16 heavily paraphrased, are also from Augustine, *De Gen. ad Lit.* iii.10.15:

Si autem transgressores illi antequam transgrederentur coelestia corpora gerebant, neque hoc mirum est, si conversa sunt ex poena in aeriam qualitatem, ut iam possint ab igne, id est ab elemento naturae superioris, aliquid pati: nec aeris saltem spatia superiora atque puriora, sed ista caliginosa tenere permissi sunt, qui eis pro suo genere quidam quasi carcer est usque ad tempus iudicii.

This may be a case in which Isidore did not have the text before him but was working from notes or even from memory. *Hi sunt . . . princeps est* is from Lactantius, *Inst. div.* ii.14.5: *Hi sunt inmundi spiritus, malorum quae geruntur auctores, quorum idem diabolus est princeps.* The *praevaricatores angeli* are to be found in Augustine, *Contra Faust.* xxii.7, a passage which Isidore quotes in §5.

18. *Diabolus Hebraice dicitur deorsum fluens, quia quietus in caeli culmine stare contempsit, sed superbiae pondere deorsum curruens cecidit. Graece vero diabolus criminator vocatur, quod vel crimina, in qua ipse inlicit, ad Deum referat, vel quia electorum innocentiam criminibus fictis accusat; unde et in Apocalypsi voce angelica dicitur (12, 10): 'Proiectus est accusator fratrum nostrorum, qui accusabat illos in conspectu Dei nostri die ac nocte.'*

The etymologies *deorsum fluens* and *criminator* for *diabolus* are from Jerome, *Comm. in Epist. ad Eph.* 6:11:

Diabolus autem nomen Graecum est, quod interpretatur criminator. Juxta Hebraei vero sermonis proprietatem, quia et tribus Zabulon quandam similitudinem huius vocabuli habet, καταρίων, id est, deorsum fluens, dici potest, quod scilicet paulatim de virtute ad vitium fluxerit et de coelestibus ad terrena corruerit.

References to both etymologies also occur elswhere in Jerome's writings (*cf. De Hebr. nom. Apoc.* D; *Comm. in Epist. ad Eph.* 4:27; *Comm. in Epist. ad Titum* 2:6). Isidore has taken considerable liberties with the passage, reversing the order or the Greek and Hebrew, omitting parts, and inserting his own *quia quietus . . . cecidit,* perhaps inspired by a passage in Augustine, *Contra Secund. Manich.* 17 (*superbiae tumore dejectus est*). The reversal of the order of the Hebrew and Greek etymologies and the words *Graece vero* probably come from Eucherius, *Instruct.* ii, De idol.: *Diabolus deorsum fluens, Graece vero criminator dicitur. Quod vel . . . referat* is from Lactantius, *Inst. div.* ii.8.6: *Hunc ergo ex bono per se malum effectum Graeci* διάβολον *appellant; nos criminatorem vocamus, quod crimina, in quae ipse illicit, ad deum deferat.* The rest of the sentence follows the pattern of alternate explanations that Isidore is so fond of, and may be his own. The Vulgate text of Apocalypsis 12:10 reads *ante conspectum Dei* instead of *in conspectu Dei;* Isidore may have been using a variant text.

19. *Satanas in Latino sonat adversarius, sive transgressor. Ipse est enim adversarius, qui est veritatis inimicus, et semper sanctorum virtutibus contraire nititur. Ipse et transgressor, quia praevaricator effectus in veritate, qua conditus est, non stetit. Idem et temptator, quia temptandam iustorum innocentiam postulat, sicut in Iob scribitur.*

Although the definition *adversarius/transgressor* for the Hebrew *Satanas* is to be found in several places in Jerome's writings—cf. *Liber de Hebr. nom.* III Reg., Job, Luca, Apoc., Epist. Barn., Epist. ad Thes., Epist. ad Cor.; *Comm. in Matth.* 16:22–23— Isidore's immediate source in this case, judging from the almost identical wording, is Eucherius, *Instruct.* ii, De idol.: *Satanas in Latinum sonat adversarius sive transgressor.* I find no source for the remainder of this section.

20. *Antichristus appellatur quia contra Christum venturus est. Non, quomodo quidam simplices intellegunt, Antichristum ideo dictum quod ante Christum venturus sit, id est post eum veniat Christus. Non sic, sed Antichristus Graece dicitur, quod est Latine contrarius Christo.* 'Αντί *enim Graece in Latino contra significat.*

Antichristus appellatur . . . est appears to be an amalgamation of Lactantius, *Inst. div.* vii.19.6 (*hic est autem qui appellatur Antichristus*) and Augustine, *De civ. Dei* xx.19, quoting I Joh. 2:18: *Pueri, novissima hora est, et sicut audistis quod Antichristus sit venturus, nunc autem Antichristi multi facti sunt* (cf. also Jerome, *Epist.* cxxii.11). What follows appears to be Isidore's rebuke to the *simplices; cf.* §14.

21. *Christum enim mentietur, dum venerit; et contra eum dimicabitur; et adversabitur sacramentis Christi, ut veritatis eius evangelium solvat.*

Another section of dubious antecedents. The first sentence is probably from Lactantius, *Inst. div.* vii.19.6, which Isidore began to quote in §20: *hic est autem qui appellatur Antichristus, sed se ipse Christum mentietur et contra verum dimicabit et victus effugiet.*

Other references to the mendacious nature of Antichrist appear in Jerome, *Epist.* xxii Ad Eustoch. 38 and Augustine, *De civ. Dei.* xx.19. I find no source for the rest of the section.

22. *Nam et templum Hierosolymis reparare, et omnes veteris legis caerimonias restaurare temptabit. Sed et ille Antichristus est qui negat esse Deum Christum. Contrarius enim Christo est. Omnes enim, qui exeunt de Ecclesia et ab unitate fidei praeciduntur, et ipsi Antichristi sunt.*

The idea of Antichrist rebuilding the temple at Jerusalem seems to be original with Isidore, although both Jerome (*Epist.* cxxii.11) and Augustine (*De civ. Dei* xx.19) describe him as sitting there. The ultimate source of the Antichrists who depart from the church is I Joh. 2:18: *nunc autem Antichristi multi facti sunt; unde cognoscimus quod novissima sit hora. Ex nobis exierunt; sed non erant ex nobis. Quod si fuissent ex nobis, permansissent utique nobiscum.* Isidore, however, seems to have pieced the section together from several references to this text: Tertullian, *De praescr. haer.* xxxiii.11 (*At in epistula eos maxime antichristos vocat qui Christum negarent in carnem venisse*) and Augustine, *De bapt. contra Donat.* vii.15.29 (*unde et antichristi appellantur, quia Christo contrarii sunt*) and *De civ. Dei* xx.19 (*exierunt multi haeretici de medio ecclesiae, quos multos dicit Antichristos*).

23. *Bel idolum Babylonium est, quod interpretatur vetus. Fuit enim hic Belus pater Nini, primus rex Assyriorum, quem quidam Saturnum appellant; quod nomen et apud Assyrios et apud Afros postea cultum est, unde et lingua Punica Bal deus dicitur. Apud Assyrios autem Bel vocatur quadam sacrorum suorum ratione et Saturnus et Sol.*

Bel idolum . . . Sol appears to be a case where Isidore has taken the arrangement of his paragraph and much of his wording from Eucherius, then gone to Eucherius' sources for amplification. Eucherius, *Instruct.* ii, De idol., has *Beel, quod interpretatur vetustas, idolum est Babyllonium; fuit vero hic idem Belus pater Nini, regis Assyriorum.* He in turn has taken *idolum Babylonium* from Jerome, *De situ et nom. loc. Hebr.* Reg. B: *Bel, idolum Babylonium,* and *vetustas* from Jerome, *Liber de Hebr. nom.* Isaia B, Ierem. B, or Dan B: *Bel. vetustas.* His reference to Ninus is from either Jerome, *Comm. in Ezech.* 23:11–12 (*Belis Assyriorum religio est consecrata in honorem patris a Nino Beli filio*), or Augustine, *De civ. Dei* xviii.2 (*Ninus ergo iam secundus rex erat Assyriorum, qui patri suo Belo successerat regni illius regi*); the rest he quotes, or rather misquotes, from Servius, *Aen.* i.729:

QUAM BELUS. primus rex Assyriorum, ut supra diximus, quos constat Saturnum, quem et Solem dicunt,

Iunonemque coluisse, quae numina etiam apud Afros postea culta sunt. unde et lingua Punica Bal deus dicitur. Apud Assyrios, autem, Bel dicitur quadam sacrorum ratione et Saturnus et Sol.

Isidore has drawn on Servius for everything in the section beyond *Assyriorum*, and has restored the epithet *rex Assyriorum* to Belus, as it is in Servius. He has, however, omitted the reference to Juno, and changed *quae numina* to *quod nomen*, perhaps influenced by the reference to a language (*lingua Punica*). For Bel/Baal being identified with Saturn, see Jerome, *Comm. in Isaia* 46:1–2 (*quem Graeci Belum, Latini Saturnum vocant*). Excavations in North Africa indicate that there at least Baal was associated with Saturn (Cumont, *PW*, 'Balcaranensis'). Servius (*Aen.* i.642) connects him with Sol because, he says, Bel is from *El*, "sun," from which comes Greek Ἥλιος (actually, like the name *Baal* itself, *El* means "lord").

24. *Belphegor interpretatur simulacrum ignominiae. Idolum enim fuit Moab, cognomento Baal, super montem Phegor, quem Latini Priapum vocant, deum hortorum.*

This section is originally from Jerome, *De situ et nom. Hebr.* Num. et Deut. B: *Beelphegor quod interpretatur simulacrum ignominiae. Est autem idolum Moab, cognomento Baal, super montem Phogor (quem Latini Priapum vocant....).* Eucherius, *Instruct.* ii De idol., quotes Jerome virtually word for word, except that he leaves out the etymology of Belphegor from Baal and Mt. Phogor: *Beelphegor quod interpretatur simulacrum ignominiae, idolum est. Mob. hunc Latini Priapum appellant* (the curious punctuation can be laid to the editor of Eucherius, who must not have been aware of his source, and the even more curious spelling *Mob* to the ignorance of a copyist). Since Isidore includes the etymology and otherwise follows Jerome's wording rather than Eucherius' (*quem* instead of *hunc*, *vocant* instead of *appellant*), it is evident that he took this passage directly from Jerome, although he has changed Jerome's *est* to *fuit* to indicate that Beelphegor's days of glory are over. The addition of *deum hortorum* after Priapus is a characteristic Isidorian explication. For Beelphegor/Priapus, *cf.* also Jerome, *Comm. in Osee* 4:14 and 9:10.

25. *Fuit autem de Lampsaco civitate Hellesponti, de qua pulsus est; et propter virilis membri magnitudinem in numero deorum suorum eum Graeci transtulerunt, et in numen sacraverunt hortorum; unde et dicitur praeesse hortis propter eorum fecunditatem.*

This entire section is quoted from Servius, *Georg.* iv.111:

hic autem Priapus fuit de Lampsaco civitate Hellesponti, de qua pulsus est propter virilis membri magnitudinem.

post in numerum deorum receptus, meruit esse numen hortorum. . . . dicitur autem praeesse hortis propter eorum fecunditatem: . . .

One point of interest here is that Isidore's text, as it appears in Lindsay and Arevalo, has altered the application of the words *virilis membri magnitudinem*. Although Isidore may have intended to point up the depravity of paganism, it is more likely that the change is the result of scribal error and modern punctuation. Some manuscripts read *proper* instead of *et propter*, and this agrees with Servius. I think that *et* should be deleted and the semicolon placed after *magnitudinem*. Isidore has added the reference to *Graeci* and changed *meruit esse*, which he may have found objectionable, to *eum . . . in numen sacraverunt hortorum*. For Priapus as the god of gardens and a fertility deity, see also Servius, *Ecl.* vii.33, and Lactantius, *Inst. div.* i.21.30.

26. *Belzebub idolum fuit Accaron, quod interpretatur vir muscarum. Zebub enim musca vocatur. Spurcissimum igitur idolum ideo virum muscarum vocatum propter sordes idolatriae, sive pro inmunditia. Belial * * .*

The source for this section is Jerome, *Comm. in Matth.* 10:25,

Beelzebub idolum est Accaron quod vocatur in Regum volumine idolum muscae. Beel ipse est bel sive baal, zebub autem musca dicitur. Principem ergo daemoniorum exspurcissimi idoli appellabant vocabulo qui musca dicitur propter inmunditiam quae exterminat suavitatem olei.

and either *Interp. Hebr. Nom.* Evang. Joh. B or *Comm. in Eccl.* 10:1 (*vir muscarum*). Eucherius (*Instruct.* ii. De idol.) has *Beelzebub interpretatur vir muscarum*, which indicates that he also used Jerome for his source. This may be the source of Isidore's *interpretatur*, though he has also used Jerome. He has once more converted the *est* in Jerome to *fuit* (*cf.* §24), and he has eliminated the reference to the 'Prince of Demons'; the *sordes idolatriae* also seems to be his own contribution. Ecclesiastes 10:1, referred to by Jerome above, is the source of the proverbial 'fly in the ointment'. For some reason, nothing is written under the rubric for Belial. While it is impossible to anticipate with certainty what Isidore would have written, the material, as for most of the Hebrew names in this chapter, would probably have come from Jerome.

27. *Behemoth ex Hebraea voce in Latina lingua animal sonat, propter quod de excelsis ad terrena cecidit, et pro merito suo ut animal brutum effectus sit. Ipse est et Leviathan, id est serpens de aquis, quia in huius saeculi mare volubili versatur astutia.*

The reference to Behemoth is from Gregory the Great, Moralia xxxii.16 (Job 12:10): *Quem sub Behemoth nomine antiquum hostem insinuat, qui in-*

terpretatus ex Hebraea voce, in Latina lingua animal sonat? Isidore retains the connection between Behemoth and Satan, but the account of his fall to earth and conversion to a brute animal may be Isidore's own; the idea of just deserts is introduced here, as it was eliminated from the section on Priapus (§25). (*Cf.*, however, Jerome, *Comm. in Epist. ad Eph.* 4:11: *scilicet paulatim de virtute ad vitium fluxerit, et de coelestibus ad terrena corruerit.*) The 'serpent of the waters' is also from *Moralia*, xxxiii.30 (Job 15:24): *Leviathan vero, quia hamo capitur, procul dubio serpens in aquis innotescitur.* For the rest of the passage I could find no source.

28. *Leviathan autem interpretatur additamentum eorum. Quorum scilicet, nisi hominum quibus in paradiso semel culpam praevaricationis intulit, et hanc usque ad aeternam mortem cottidie persuadendo adicit vel extendit?*

Leviathan/additamentum eorum appears first in Jerome, *Interp. Hebr. nom.* Job L: *Leviathan additamentum eorum.* Isidore's source for the whole passage, however, was Gregory the Great, *Moralia* xxxiii.17 (Job 9:20): *Leviathan quippe additamentum eorum dicitur. Quorum videlicet, nisi hominum? quibus semel culpam praevaricationis intulit, et hanc usque ad aeternam mortem quotidie pessimis suggestionibus extendit.* Isidore has added *in paradiso* by way of clarification, converted *pessimis suggestionibus* to *persuadendo*, and inserted *adicit* to explain *extendit.*

29. *Quaedam autem nomina deorum suorum gentiles per vanas fabulas ad rationes physicas conantur traducere, eaque in causis elementorum conposita esse interpretantur. Sed hoc a poetis totum fictum est, ut deos suos ornarent aliquibus figuris, quod perditos ac dedecoris infamia plenos fuisse historiae confitentur. Omnino enim fingendi locus vacat, ubi veritas cessat.*

This bit of moralizing is probably Isidore's own. It contains expressions from Lactantius (*Inst. div.* 1.12.3, *quam tamen Stoici ut solent ad rationem physicam conantur traducere;* i.11.30, *Nihil igitur a poetis in totum fictum est*), but Isidore has adapted them for his own purposes, even changing the sense to the exact opposite. This is, for Isidore, an unusually severe condemnation of the pagan poets; elsewhere in the *Origines*, they are presented as misguided but well-intentioned, adorning actual persons and events with figures of speech in order to enhance the glory of their subject; see in particular §2, and also *Origines* viii.7.2 (*Igitur ut templa illis domibus pulchriora, et simulacra corporibus ampliora faciebant, ita eloquio etiam quasi augustiore honorandos putaverunt laudesque eorum et verbis inlustrioribus et iucundioribus numeris extulerunt*) and viii.7.10 (*Officium autem poetae in eo est ut ea, quae vere gesta sunt, in alias species obliquis figurationibus cum decore aliquo*

conversa transducant). But to the extent that their pleasant fictions make gods out of men, Isidore condems them, like Lactantius before him (*cf. Inst. div.* i.11 *passim*), for leading men into error.

30. *Saturnus origo deorum et totius posteritatis a paganis designatur. Hunc Latini a satu appellatum ferunt, quasi ad ipsum satio omnium pertineat rerum, vel a temporibus longitudine, quod saturetur annis.*

With §30 begins Isidore's discussion of the pagan gods proper, those whom Augustine, quoting Varro (*De civ. Dei* vii.2), designates "select gods":

Hos certe deos selectos Varro unius libri contextione commendat: Ianum, Iovem, Saturnum, Genium, Mercurium, Apollinem, Martem, Vulcanum, Neptunum, Solem, Orcum, Liberum patrem, Tellurem, Cererem, Iunonem, Lunam, Dianam, Minervam, Venerem, Vestam.

Isidore follows the list (though not the order) fairly closely, deviating from it only to conflate some of the gods (Apollo/Sol, Diana/Luna/Proserpina, and, somewhat illogically, Ceres/Proserpina/Vesta/Tellus), and to consign Genius, who by that time had lost his importance as a symbol of the imperial authority, to the collection of minor gods, Egyptian deities, demigods, spooks, and monsters with which he ends the chapter.

Isidore begins appropriately with Saturn, the ancestor of the Olympian gods. The first sentence of the section is taken from Tertullian, *Ad nat.* ii.12: *Origo enim totius posteritatis. Ea origo deorum vestrorum Saturno, ut opinor, signatur.* Isidore has changed the passage from direct address to third person narrative, and so deletes *vestrorum* and inserts *a paganis*; otherwise he follows Tertullian quite closely. The derivation of *Saturnus* from *satu* is to be found in Varro, *L.L.* v.64, *ab satu est dictus Saturnus;* either this passage or another similar one in Varro may have been Isidore's ultimate source. (*Cf.* also Tertullian, *Ad nat.* ii.12, *aeque Latini vocabuli a sationibus rationem.*) *Latini* is probably Isidore's addition, and *quasi ad . . . rerum* is a characteristic Isidorian amplification. The reference to *temporis longitudo* is from Augustine, *De civ. Dei* iv.10: *Quia Saturnus, inquiunt, temporis longitudo est.* The derivation of his name from *saturetur annis* appears in both Augustine, *De cons. evang.* i.23 (*unde Latine Saturnus appellatur, quasi saturetur annis*) and Lactantius, *Inst. div.* i.12.9 (*Saturnus autem est appellatus quod saturetur annis*). Both were drawing upon Cicero, *De nat. deor.* ii.24.64: *Saturnus autem est appellatus quod saturaretur annis;* . . . The first etymology, from *satus*, appears to be correct, although efforts have been made to connect *Saturnus* with an Etruscan root (see Thulin, *PW*, 'Saturnus'). The second is an attempt to establish a connection with time for the Latin Saturnus, because he was identified with the Greek Κρόνος, whose name was thought to be derived from χρόνος (see §31).

31. *Unde et eum Graeci Cronos nomen habere dicunt, id est tempus, quod filios suos fertur devorasse, hoc est annos, quos tempus produxerit, in se revolvit, vel quod eo semina, unde oriuntur, iterum redeunt.*

The immediate sources for this section are Servius, *Aen.* iii.104 (*ut autem fingatur Saturnus filios suos comesse, ratio haec est, quia dicitur deus esse aeternitatis et saeculorum. Saecula autem annos ex se natos in se revolvunt: unde Graece* Κρόνος *quasi* Χρόνος, *id est tempus, dicitur. Cf.* also Lactantius, *Inst. div.* i.12.9) and Augustine, *De civ. Dei* vi.8 (*vel, sicut idem opinatur Varro, quod pertineat Saturnus ad semina, quae in terram, de qua oriuntur, iterum recidunt. Cf.* also *De civ. Dei* vii.19). The etymology of Κρόνος from χρόνος, which led to the identification of both Saturn and Kronos with Father Time, is a very ancient one, and by far the most popular of several derivations current among the Greeks, including a possibly correct one from κραίνω, although it is more likely that the name, as well as the god, is prehellenic. See Pohlenz, *PW*, "Kronos." It appears in Cicero, *De nat. deor.* ii.25.64: Κρόνος *enim dicitur, qui est idem* Χρόνος, *id est spatium temporis. Saturnus autem est appellatus quod saturaretur annis; ex se enim natos comesse fingitur solitus, quia consumit aetas temporum spatia, annisque praeteritis insaturabiliter expletur.* This is the source of Lactantius, *Inst. div.* i.12.9, and probably also of Augustine, *De civ. Dei* vii.19, and Servius, *Aen.* iii.104, mentioned above.

32. *Hunc Caeli patris abscidisse genitalia dicunt, quia nihil in caelo de seminibus nascitur. Falcem tenet, inquiunt, propter agriculturam significandam, vel propter annos et tempora, quod in se redeant, vel propter sapientiam, quod intus acuta sit.*

The first sentence of this section is a combination of Lactantius, *Inst. div.* i.12.2–3 (*deinde, quod ne iustus quidem fuit, sed impius non modo in filios, quos necavit, verum etiam in patrem, cuius dicitur abscidisse genitalia, . . .*) and Augustine (quoting Varro), *De civ. Dei* vii.19 (*Hoc propterea, quantum intellegi datur, quia nihil in caelo de seminibus nascitur*). Also from Augustine/Varro (*De civ. Dei* vii.19) comes the scythe symbolic of agriculture ("*Falcem habet,*" *inquit,* "*propter agriculturam.*"); *vel propter . . . redeant* is from Servius, *Georg.* ii.406 (*alii Saturnum deum esse temporum dicunt, quae, sicut falx, in se recurrunt*). There appears to be no extant source of the scythe as symbol of wisdom (because it is "sharp on the inside"); the analogy is so recherché that I suspect Isidore of having invented it.

33. *In aliquibus autem civitatibus Saturno liberos suos apud gentiles inmolabant, quod Saturnum poetae liberos suos devorasse solitum tradiderunt.*

The sources for this section are Jerome, *Comm. in Isaiam* 46:1–2 (*quem Graeci Belum, Latini Saturnum*

vocant. Cuius tanta fuit apud veteres religio ut ei non solum humanas hostias captivorum ignobiliumque mortalium, sed et suos liberos immolarent) and Augustine, *De civ. Dei* iv.27 (*sic item aliquid aliter, turpiter atque inepte dicere ac facere, . . . Saturnum liberos devorare*). Using the latter to explain the former seems to be Isidore's own idea, although a somewhat similar explanation is to be found in Lactantius, *Inst. div.* i.21.9: *nam de infantibus qui eidem Saturno immolabantur propter odium Iovis, quid dicam non invenio . . .* Child sacrifice among the Tyrians and Carthaginians, of course, had nothing to do with the Greek myth; it was part of their worship of Baal/El, whom the Greeks associated with Kronos and the Romans with Saturn (see Pohlenz, *PW*, "Kronos"). The grim practice is well attested by both pagan and Christian writers (see Diodorus Siculus, xx.14; Tertullian, *Apol.* ix.2; Minucius Felix, *Oct.* xxx.3), as well as the Old Testament (Jer. 19:1–5). Archaeological evidence came to light early in this century, when the Tophet at Carthage was excavated and urns were found containing the charred bones of human infants (see *CAH*, **VIII**: pp. 491–492; D. B. Harden, "The Topography of Punic Carthage," *Greece and Rome*, **IX** (October, 1939): pp. 5–6).

34. *Iovis fertur a iuvando dictus, et Iuppiter quasi iuvans pater, id est, omnibus praestans. Hunc et privato titulo Iovem Optimum dixerunt, dum fuisset incestus in suis, inpudicus in extraneis.*

Iovis fertur . . . praestans: One or the other of these etymologies occurs in several places; Isidore has combined Lactantius, *Inst. div.* i.11.40 (*Iovem enim Iunonemque a iuvando esse dictos Cicero interpretatur et Iuppiter quasi iuvans pater dicitur. Cf.* Cicero *De nat. deor.* ii.25.64) and Servius, *Aen.* ix.126 (*IUPPITER IPSE. scilicet qui omnibus praestare consuevit: unde et Iuppiter dictus est, quasi iuvans pater*). They are, incidentally, not so mistaken as one might think. That *-piter* is derived from *pater* is an obvious deduction to anyone familiar with the pattern of vowel weakening in Latin; and although the root *iu-* or *iov-* is not from *iuvare* but from Indo-European *djo-*, "bright" or "shining," an appropriate epithet for a sky god, and cognate with *dies* and *deus* (*cf.* Varro, *L.L.* v.66), *iuvare* itself may come from this same root. *Hunc et privato . . . dixerunt* is probably from Lactantius, *Inst. div.* i.10.10 (*quid horum omnium pater Iuppiter, qui in sollemni precatione Optimus Maximus nominatur*). I discovered no immediate source for the remainder of the section, although sentiments of this sort are expressed throughout the patristic writers.

35. *Quem modo taurum fingunt propter Europae raptum; fuit enim in navi cuius insigne erat taurus: modo Danaes per imbrem aureum appetisse concubitum; ubi intellegitur pudicitiam mulieris ab auro fuisse cor-*

ruptam: modo in similitudine aquilae, propter quod puerum ad stuprum rapuerit: modo serpentem, quia reptaverit, et cygnum, quia cantaverit.

The references to Europa, Danae, and Ganymede are from Lactantius, *Inst. div.* i.11.18–19,

Danaen violaturus aureos nummos largiter in sinum eius infudit, haec stupri merces fuit. at poetae, qui quasi de deo loquebantur, ne auctoritatem creditae maiestatis infringerent, finxerunt ipsum in aureo imbre delapsum eadem figura qua imbres ferreos dicunt cum multitudinem telorum sagittarumque describunt. rapuisse dicitur in aquila Catamitum: poeticus color est. sed aut per legionem rapuit cuius insigne aquila est, aut navis in qua est inpositus tutelam habuit in aquila figuratam, sicut taurum, cum rapuit et transvexit Europam.

and Augustine, *De civ. Dei* xviii.13,

Porro autem quicumque finxerunt a Iove ad stuprum raptum pulcherrimum puerum Ganymedem, quod nefas rex Tantalus fecit et Iovi fabula tribuit, vel Danaes per imbrem aureum adpetisse concubitum, ubi intellegitur pudicitia mulieris auro fuisse corrupta, quae illis temporibus vel facta vel ficta sunt, . . .

The passage on Danae is quoted verbatim from Augustine; the others are paraphrases, the first from Lactantius, which Isidore expands and reworks considerably, the other a combination of material from both passages and possibly also from Lactantius i.10.12 (*illud vero summae impietatis ac sceleris, quod regium puerum rapuit ad stuprum*). There appears to be no immediate source for *modo serpentem . . . cantaverit*. The swan, of course, figures in the story of Leda; swans were noted in antiquity for their ability to sing (see Ovid, *Met.* v.386–387; Vergil, *Aen.* i.393–400; Horace, *Carm.* iv.3.19–20). The serpent disguise, which Jupiter used to seduce Proserpina in the myth of Zagreus, is mentioned in Ovid, *Met.* vi.112–113 (*aureus ut Danaen, Asopida luserit ignis,/Memnosynen pastor, varius Deoida serpens*), which may be where Isidore learned of it. It appears that he is applying the euhemerism of Lactantius and Augustine to a couple of myths of his own choice.

36. *Et ideo non figurae istae sunt, sed plane de veritate scelera. Unde turpe erat tales deos credi, quales homines esse non debeant.*

The first sentence of this section appears to be Isidore's own restatement of the all too human and sinful nature of the pagan gods. *Unde turpe . . . debeant* is taken from Tertullian, *Ad nat.* ii.7 (*ridendum an irascendum sit, tales deos credi quales homines esse non debeant?*); cf. Lactantius, *Inst. div.* i.11.1.

37. *Ianum dicunt quasi mundi vel caeli vel mensuum ianuam: duas Iani facies faciunt, propter orientem et occidentem. Cum vero faciunt eum quadrifrontem et Ianum geminum appellant, ad quattuor mundi partes*

hoc referunt, vel ad quattuor elementa sive tempora. Sed dum hoc fingunt, monstrum, non deum faciunt.

The derivation of *Ianus* from *ianua* (actually, they both come from a common root connected with *eo, ire*, "to go") is to be found in Tertullian, *De idol.* 15 (*et ipsum Ianum a ianua*). His association with *mundus* is mentioned by several authors, any of whom could have been Isidore's source (cf. Augustine, *De civ. Dei* vii.7–9; Servius, *Aen.* vii.610), although they generally speak of him as being the universe itself rather than the gateway to it. *Vel caeli* appears to be Isidore's explanation for *mundi*. For *mensuum* Arevalo has *mensium*, which is surely the correct reading, even though none of the extant manuscripts support it; cf. Augustine, *De civ. Dei* vii.7. January, the month of Janus, is the first month of the year, and so the "gateway of the months." *Cum vero . . . referunt* is from Augustine, *De civ. Dei* vii.8 (*cum vero eum faciunt quadrifrontem et Ianum geminum appellant, ad quattuor mundi partes hoc interpretatur. Cf.* also Servius, *Aen.* vii.610). The reference to the four seasons is in Servius, *Aen.* vii.610 (*Ianum sane apud aliquos bifrontem, apud aliquos quadrifrontem esse non mirum est: nam alii eum diei dominum volunt in quo ortus est et occassus, . . . alii anni totius quem in quattuor tempora constat esse divisum*). The association of Janus with the four elements appears to be Isidore's invention. Augustine, *De civ. Dei* vii.4, makes mention of the monstrous appearance of Janus' images (*eum simulacri monstrosa deformitate turpaverunt, nunc eum bifrontem, nunc quadrifrontem, tamquam geminum facientes*), and this is probably the source of Isidore's concluding remarks.

38. *Neptunum aquas mundi praedicant; et dictus ab eis Neptunus, quasi nube tonans.*

Isidore's source for *Neptunum aquas mundi praedicant* is Augustine, *De civ. Dei* vii.16: *volunt . . . Neptunum aquas mundi.* There is no extant source for the etymology from *nube tonans*, but it probably goes back ultimately to Varro, who astutely made the connection between the root *nub-* of *nubes* and the *nep-* of *Neptunus* (*L.L.* v.72). The *compositio* from a participial phrase is on a par with *Mercurius* from *medius currens* (see §45) and those etymologies of Varro's that so amazed and delighted Quintilian (*Inst.* i.6.37).

39. *Vulcanum volunt ignem; et dictus Vulcanus quasi volans candor, vel quasi volicanus, quod per aerem volat. Ignis enim e nubibus nascitur.*

Vulcanum volunt ignem is from Augustine, *De civ. Dei* vii.16: *Vulcanum volunt ignem mundi, Neptunum aquas mundi, . . .* Isidore omits the *mundi*. The rest of the section, with the exception of *volans candor,* is from Servius, *Aen.* viii.414: *IGNIPOTENS. Vulcanus, ut diximus (i.171), ignis est, et dictus*

Vulcanus quasi Volcanus, quod per aerem volet; ignis enim e nubibus nascitur. Where, if anywhere, Isidore found the etymology from *volans candor* is a mystery; Servius draws the analogy only between *Volcanus* and *volare.* The use of *compositio* with a participle suggests Varro, but Varro (*L.L.* v.70) derives *Vulcanus* from *vi ac violentia.* It is possible that Isidore himself invented it in an inspired moment. (For a different but equally exotic derivation, see Fulgentius, *Virg. Con.* 164.) In fact, the name *Vulcanus* does perhaps mean "the bright one," not because it has anything to do with *candor* but because it comes from the root *vulc-* (*folc-, fulc-*), "shining"; *cf. fulgeo, fulgor, fulvus.*

40. *Unde et Homerus dicit eum praecipitatum de aere in terras, quod omne fulmen de aere cadit. Idcirco autem Vulcanus de femore Iunonis fingitur natus, quod fulmina de imo aere nascantur.*

Isidore took *unde enim . . . cadit* from Servius, *Aen.* viii.414, *unde etiam Homerus dicit eum de aere praecipitatum in terras, quod omne fulmen de aere cadit.* (The passage in Homer referred to is *Iliad* i.590–594.) Isidore seems to have regarded Vulcan (on the basis of Servius) as a lightning god. Servius is also the source (*Aen.* vii.454) of the bizarre story of Vulcan's birth from the thigh of Juno: *ideo autem Vulcanus de femore Iunonis fingitur natus, quod fulmina de imo aere nascuntur:* . . . It is probably a doublet of the story of the birth of Dionysus from the thigh of Zeus; in one version of the myth (Hesiod, *Theog.* 927ff.) Hera is supposed to have given birth to Hephaestus without benefit of a father, but in retaliation for the birth of Athena, not Dionysus.

41. *Claudus autem dicitur Vulcanus, quia per naturam numquam rectus est ignis, sed quasi claudus eiusmodi speciem motumque habet. Ideo autem in fabrorum fornace eundem Vulcanum auctorem dicunt, quia sine igne nullum metalli genus fundi extendique potest.*

The sources of *claudus autem . . . habet* are Servius, *Aen.* viii.414 (*claudus autem dicitur, quia per naturam numquam rectus est ignis*) and Augustine, *Contra Faust.* xx.9 (*Sicut Vulcanum claudum, quia ignis terreni motus eiusmodi est*). This explanation for the smith-god's lameness was popular in antiquity (see L. Martin, *PW*, "Hephaistos"); but the real reason may be more practical than symbolic: smithing would be a usual occupation for a lame but otherwise robust man in a primitive society (*OCD*, "Hephaestus"). *Ideo autem . . . dicunt* is from Augustine, *De civ. Dei* iv.11, *in fabrorum fornace Vulcanus.* I find no source for the rest of the section; however, Isidore quotes it again at *Origines* xix.6.2.

42. *Pluton Graece, Latine Diespiter vel Ditis pater; quem Orcum vocant, quasi receptorem mortium. Unde*

et orca nuncupatur vas quod recipit aquas. Ipse et Graece Charon.

Pluton Graece . . . vocant is from Lactantius, *Inst. div.* i.14.5: *Pluto Latine est Dis pater, alii Orcum vocant.* The problem of *Diespiter,* which is normally a title of Jupiter, not Pluto, apparently goes back to the text of Lactantius (the text used above has been emended to *Dis pater* from *Diespiter* by the modern editor). *Cf.* the note to this passage in the text in Migne, *PL* Vol. VI, Col. 190:

In multis mss. et in omnibus fere editis est Diespiter: quod Iovis, non Plutonis cognomen est, teste Macrobio Saturnal. i. cap. 15. Pluto latine sonat *Dis;* et sic vocatus est Aeneid lib. vi v.269, id est *dives.* Pluto, autem (ut notat Cicero lib. ii, de Nat. deorum), est Dispater, quasi dicas *pater dives,* vel, *Deus divitiarum:* Quia *Dis* ut apud Graecos, Πλούτων. . . . Qua autem ratione in caeteris Lactantii mss. et editis vacatur Diespiter non video. Nomen enim Diespitris Iovi attributum fuisse notissimum est; at Plutoni numquam quod sciam.

A similar difficulty is to be found in Varro, *L.L.* v.66, where the title of Jupiter is given as Dispiter and emended to *Diespiter* by Laetus. This was probably not the source of Lactantius' difficulty, but it does indicate that confusion existed in the Middle Ages concerning the two names. Isidore appears to have inserted *Ditis pater.* It is hard to say what he meant by it; the nominative *Ditis* does occur (see Quintilian, i.6.34), but it is also possible that Isidore intended it as a genitive: "Father of wealth." Pluto's role as *receptor mortium* is from Augustine, *De civ. Dei* vii.3: *nullum eis* [sc. *Menti, Virtuti, Felicitati*] *locum inter selectos deos dare voluerunt ubi dederunt Marti et Orco, uni effectori mortium, alteri receptori.* I do not know where Isidore discovered the derivation of *orca* from *Orcus;* there does not seem to be any relationship between the two. According to Festus, the *orca,* actually a sort of barrel, was so named because in shape it was "very like a whale." Although in classical myth Charon was the boatman who ferried the dead across to Hades, in late antiquity he came to be associated with Death and the god of the dead (see Schwartz, *PW*, "Charon"). This may be due in part to confusion with the Etruscan demon Charun.

43. *Liberum a liberamento appellatum volunt, quod quasi mares in coeundo per eius beneficium emissis seminibus liberentur; quod idem Liber muliebri et delicato corpore pingitur. Dicunt enim mulieres ei adtributas et vinum propter excitandam libidinem.*

Liberum . . . liberentur and *Dicunt enim . . . libidinem* are taken from Augustine, *De civ. Dei* vi.9: *Liberum a liberamento appellatum volunt, quod mares in coeundo per eius beneficium emissis seminibus liberentur:* . . . *Ad haec addunt mulieres attributas Libero, et vinum propter libidinem excitandam.*

Augustine is in turn quoting Varro. *Quod idem
. . . pingitur* is from Eusebius/Jerome, *Chron.* An.
dccxxiv: *pingitur vero Liber muliebri et delicato corpore
propter mulieres in suo exercitu militantes, . . .*
Isidore quotes the reference to Liber's effeminate
appearance, but connects it only with women as a
means of arousing lust in men, not with female
warriors; he regards Liber primarily as a god of lust.
The similarity between the god's name and the
adjective *liber* was so obvious that a number of
ingenious but incorrect attempts were made to
relate them (*cf.* Servius, *Aen.* iv.58; *Georg.* i.66).
Varro's reflects Liber's original role as a fertility
god. The name, as Festus correctly observes (*De
sig. verb.* 108L), is actually cognate with Greek λοιβή
and λείβειν and with Latin *libare*, "to pour a libation."

44. *Unde et frons eius pampino cingitur. Sed ideo
coronam viteam et cornu habet, quia cum grate et
moderate vinum bibitur, laetitiam praestat; cum ultra
modum, excitat lites, id est quasi cornua dat. Idem
autem et Lyaeus ἀπὸ τοῦ λύειν, quod multo vino membra
solvantur. Iste et Graece Διόνυσος a monte Indiae
Nysa, ubi dicitur esse nutritus. Ceterum est et Nysa
civitas, in qua colitur idem Liber, unde Nysaeus
dictus est.*

Although there are references in classical authors,
notably in Horace (*cf. Carm.* ii.19.30; iv.8.33) to
Dionysus/Liber horned or crowned with vine leaves,
I discovered no source for Isidore's interpretation of
the symbolic meaning of these attributes. Horace
(*Carm.* iii.21.18) speaks of wine giving *cornua
pauperi*, but that appears to be a desirable effect.
Idem autem . . . solvantur is taken from Servius,
Aen. iv.58: *PATRIQUE LYAEO. dictus Lyaeos
ἀπὸ τοῦ λύειν, quod nimio vino membra solvantur.* The
etymology is correct. The association of Dionysus
with Mt. Nysa is an ancient one; the ultimate source
for this reference may be Varro, but it is conceivable
that Isidore worked it out for himself from the
passage in Servius that follows (*Aen.* vi.805).
Actually, Dionysus' name is probably from the root
dyo- or *djo-* already encountered in *Iuppiter*, and a
Thracian root *νυσο-*, meaning "child" (see Kern, *PW*,
"Dionysos"). The remainder of the section is from
Servius, *Aen.* vi.805: *NYSAE DE VERTICE.
Mons est Indiae, de quo loquitur. ceterum est et Nysa
civitas, in qua Liber colitur, unde Nysaeus dictus est.*

45. *Mercurium sermonem interpretantur. Nam ideo
Mercurius quasi medius currens dicitur appellatus,
quod sermo currat inter homines medius. Ideo et
'Ερμῆς Graece, quod sermo, vel interpretatio, quae ad
sermonem utique pertinet, ἑρμηνεία dicitur.*

This entire section was taken from Augustine,
De civ. Dei vii.14:

*Quod si sermo ipse dicitur esse Mercurius, sicut ea quae
de illo interpretantur ostendunt (nam ideo Mercurius*

*quasi medius currens dicitur appellatus, quod sermo
currat inter homines medius; ideo et 'Ερμῆς Graece, quod
sermo vel interpretatio, quae ad sermonem utique
pertinet, ἑρμηνεία dicitur; . . .*

This etymology, originally from Varro, also appears
in Servius, *Aen.* vii.138. The more sensible derivation, mentioned by Isidore in §3 above, is from *merx,
mercis* (*cf.* Servius, *Aen.* iv.638; Festus, *De sig. verb.*
111L). No satisfactory etymology has been found
for 'Ερμῆς, but it is clear that ἑρμηνεία is derived from
it (by way of ἑρμηνεύς and ἑρμηνεύω) instead of the
other way around. The derivation of *Mercurius*
from *medius currens* is yet another unsatisfactory
attempt to discover a Latin equivalent for a pair
of related (or seemingly related) Greek words, like
Saturnus from *saturetur annis*, corresponding to
Κρόνος/Χρόνος (*cf.* §§30 and 31 above).

46. *Ideo et mercibus praeesse, quia inter vendentes et
ementes sermo fit medius. Qui ideo fingitur habere
pinnas, quia citius verba discurrunt. Unde et velox
et errans inducitur: alas eius in capite et in pedibus
significare volucrem fieri per aera sermonem.*

Isidore continues to quote from Augustine, *De civ.
Dei* vii.14: *ideo et mercibus praeesse, quia inter vendentes et ementes sermo fit medius; alas eius in capite
et pedibus significare volucrem ferri per aera sermonem;
. . .* Either he or a later copyist has changed
Augustine's *ferri* to *fieri*. *Qui ideo . . . inducitur*
is inserted from Servius, *Aen.* iv.239: *TALARIA
NECTIT. Mercurius ideo dicitur habere pennas
quia citius ab omnibus planetis in ortum suum re-
currit: unde et velox et errans inducitur, ut quos ignis
caeli Cyllenius erret in orbes.* Isidore has deleted
all references to the planet Mercury (as being more
appropriate to astronomy than to religion?) and
inserted *verba discurrunt* to adapt Mercury's wings to
his role as god of speech.

47. *Nuntium dictum, quoniam per sermonem omnia
cogitata enuntiantur. Ideo autem furti magistrum
dicunt, quia sermo animos audientium fallit. Virgam
tenet, qua serpentes dividit, id est venena.*

This section is taken from Augustine, *De civ. Dei*
vii.14 (*nuntium dictum, quoniam per sermonem omnia
cogitata enuntiatur*) and Servius, *Aen.* iv.242 (*unde
virga serpentes dividit, id est venena*). The serpents
were originally the garlands or fillets ornamenting
the herald's wand; they came to be depicted as
serpents because of a myth (told by Hyginus, *P.
Astr.* ii.7) in which Hermes came upon two snakes
fighting and separated them with his staff. *Venena*
in this context seem to signify the discord quelled by
the *caduceatores*. There is no reference to Hermes as
patron of thieves in either Augustine or Servius,
although Augustine (*De civ. Dei* vii.26) does mention
his thieving: *Quid sunt ad hoc malum furta Mercurii
. . . ?* His reputation as a thief was established

in the fourth *Homeric Hymn;* Ovid recounts his deceptions, *Met.* ii.686ff., and describes him as *furibus apte (Fasti* v.104). *Cf.* also Lactantius, *Inst. div.* v.10.16.

48. *Nam bellantes ac dissidentes interpretum oratione sedantur; unde secundum Livium legati pacis caduceatores dicuntur. Sicut enim per fetiales bella indicebantur, ita pax per caduceatores fiebat.*

This entire section is from Servius, *Aen.* iv.242:

nam serpentes ideo introrsum spectantia capita habent ut significent inter se legatos colloqui et convenire debere, quia bellantes interpretum oratione sedantur: unde secundum Livium legati pacis caduceatores dicuntur: sicut enim per fetiales, a foedere, bella indicebantur, ita pax per caduceatores fiebat.

The passage in Livy has unfortunately been lost.

49. *Hermes autem Graece dicitur ἀπὸ τῆς ἑρμηνείας, Latine interpres; qui ob virtutem multarumque artium scientiam Trimegistus, id est ter maximus nominatus est. Cur autem eum capite canino fingunt, haec ratio dicitur, quod inter omnia animalia canis sagacissimum genus et perspicax habeatur.*

Hermes autem . . . interpres is also from Servius, *Aen.* iv.242: Ἑρμῆς *autem Graece dicitur ἀπὸ τῆς ἑρμηνείας, Latine interpres.* Isidore took his information on Hermes Trismegistus from Lactantius, *De ira Dei* xi.12: *qui ob virtutem multarumque artium scientiam Termaximus nominatus est.* The Greek form of his name is probably from Lactantius, *Inst. div.* i.6.3, *ut ei multarum rerum et artium scientia Trismegisto cognomen imponeret.* His dog's head is explained by Servius, *Aen.* viii.698 *LATRATOR ANUBIS. quia capite canino pingitur, hunc volunt esse Mercurium, ideo quia nihil est cane sagacius);* this is probably Isidore's source, although he does not follow the wording as closely as he usually does in Servius. Actually, the Egyptian god Anubis had a jackal's head; his identification with Mercury/ Hermes was inspired not by the natural sagacity of dogs (or jackals) but because he, like Hermes Ψυχοπομπός, conducted souls to the underworld, a not inappropriate function for a jackal god. Hermes was also identified, on the basis of his cleverness, with the ibis-headed Thoth, god of the arts and sciences, and it was in this capacity that he was known as Hermes Trismegistos.

50. *Martem deum belli esse dicunt, et Martem appellatum quia per viros pugnatur, ut sit Mars mas; licet et tria sint genera consuetudinum, sicut Scytharum, ubi et feminae et viri in pugna eunt: Amazonum, ubi solae feminae: Romanorum aliarumque gentium, ubi soli mares.*

The only part of this section that can be traced to a definite source is *Martem . . . dicunt,* which is from Augustine, *De civ. Dei* vii.14: Marti . . . deum

belli esse dixerunt. The derivation of *Mars* from *mas* occurs in Varro, *L.L.* v.73 *(Mars ab eo quod maribus in bello praeest)* ; Varro may be Isidore's ultimate source. Arevalo has emended Isidore's *ut sit Mars mas* to *ut sit Mars maris ars,* an unnecessary complication in light of the fact that Isidore derives *mas* from *Mars* (by analogy with *aries* from *Ἄρης*) at *Origines* xii.1.11. Apparently to Isidore's mind etymologies were reciprocal. Both Herodotus (iv.110– 117) and Plato *(Laws* vii.804–805) make mention of the Scythian women who went into battle with the men, but I have discovered no direct Latin source for the three styles of warfare. It may have been the lost *Historiae* of Sallust (see Dressel, "De Isidori Originum Fontibus," *Rivista di Filologia e di Instruzione Classica,* III [1875], pp. 219–220).

51. *Item Martem quasi effectorem mortium. Nam a Marte mors nuncupatur. Hunc et adulterum dicunt, quia belligerantibus incertus est.*

The source for *item Martem . . . mortium* is Augustine, *De civ. Dei* vii.3: *nullum eis locum inter selectos deos dare voluerunt, ubi dederunt Marti et Orco. uni effectori mortium, alteri receptori.* The etymology of *mors* from *Mars* can be traced no further back than Isidore; perhaps it is ultimately from Varro. Isidore cites it again at *Origines* xi.2.31. *Hunc et . . . est* is from Augustine, *Contra Faust.* xx.9 *(et Martis adulteram, quia belligerantibus incongrua est).* Augustine is referring to Venus, and remarks simply that the love goddess has no place in battle (and presumably no business being Mars's *adultera);* Isidore has made Mars the adulterer, because he is fickle to those fighting, so that the outcome of battle is uncertain. The adjective *incertus* applied to Mars is from Servius, *Aen.* ii.335: *CAECO MARTE. aut nocturno proelio; aut epithetum Martis est, cuius exitus semper incertus est.*

52. *Quod vero nudo pectore stat, ut bello se quisque sine formidine cordis obiciat. Mars autem apud Thracos Gradivus dicitur, eo quod in bello gradum inferant qui pugnant, aut quod inpigre gradiantur.*

I find no source for Mars fighting *nudo pectore,* or for Isidore's interpretation of the practice. *Mars autem . . . dicitur* may be a misunderstanding of Vergil, *Aen.* iii.35 *(Gradivum patrem, Geticis qui praesidet arvas),* coupled with Servius' commentary on the line *(GETICIS. Thraciis).* The rest of the section is also from Servius, *Aen.* iii.35: *quod gradum inferant qui pugnant; aut quod inpigre gradiantur.* Mars Gradivus was, of course, a Roman god, although he may have been identified with a similar Thracian deity. Ovid mentions him several times *(cf. Fasti* ii.861; *Met.* vi.427; xiv.820; xv.863). The epithet apparently means "he who marches forth," from *gradior.*

53. *Apollinem quamvis divinatorem et medicum vellent, ipsum tamen etiam Solem dixerunt, quasi solum. Ipsum Titan, quasi unum ex Titanis, qui adversus Iovem non fecit.*

Isidore took *Apollinem quamvis . . . dixerunt* from Augustine, *De civ. Dei* vii.16: *Apollinem quamvis divinatorem et medicum velint, tamen ut in aliqua parte mundi statuerint, ipsum etiam solem esse dixerunt.* The most likely source for his association of *Sol* and *solus* is Lactantius, *Inst. div.* ii.9 (*nam sicut sol, qui oritur in diem, licet sit unus, unde solem appellatum Cicero vult videri, quod obscuratis sideribus solus appareat*). The derivation was popular, however, and appears elsewhere. Lactantius' source was Cicero, *De nat. deor.* ii.27.68; *cf.* also Varro, *L.L.* v.68. *Ipsum Titan . . . fecit* is from Servius, *Aen.* iv.119: *TITAN. Sol: unus enim de Titanibus Hyperionis filius contra Iovem non fecit.* Isidore, like many before him, confuses Apollo with the sun god Helius or Sol. It may have been his awareness that Apollo was the son of Jupiter that caused him to omit *Hyperionis filius* from the passage in Servius.

54. *Ipsum Phoebum, quasi ephebum, hoc est adolescentem. Unde et sol puer pingitur, eo quod cottidie oriatur et nova luce nascatur. Pythium quoque eundem Apollinem vocari aiunt a Pythone inmensae molis serpente, cuius non magis venena quam magnitudo terrebat.*

55. *Hunc Apollo sagittarum ictibus sternens nominis quoque spolia reportavit, ut Pythius vocaretur. Unde et ob insigne victoriae Pythia sacra celebranda constituit.*

The curious extraction of *Phoebus* from *ephebus*, and the tradition of the sun being portrayed as a boy (which he was not, unless a man in the prime of his youth can be called a *puer*) can be traced no further back than Isidore, although it subsequently finds its way, together with other Isidorian oddities like the etymology of *Neptunus*, into the Vatican Mythographers (i.113). At *Origines* xi.2.10, Isidore extracts *ephebus* from *Phoebus*. The correct etymology of *Phoebus*, incidentally, is to be found in Macrobius, *Sat.* i.17.33 (*plerique autem a specie et nitore* Φοῖβον. *id est* καθαρὸν καὶ λαμπρὸν *dictum putant*). Isidore may have found the source for his myth of Apollo and the Python in Servius, *Aen.* iii.73, but if so he has reworked it to a degree unusual for borrowings from Servius. It is more likely that he copied the story from a source that has now been lost. The battle of Apollo and the Python is also told by Ovid, *Met.* i.438–451, and Hyginus, *Fab.* cxl. Neither of these accounts bears much resemblance to Isidore's version with regard to their wording, but the passage in Ovid at least relates the same general story that Isidore does, stressing the size and poisonous nature of the serpent, Apollo's arrows, and the

institution of the Pythian games, and making no mention of Juno or Latona.

56. *Dianam quoque germanam eius similiter lunam et viarum praesidem aiunt. Unde et virginem volunt, quod via nihil pariat. Et ideo ambo sagittas habere finguntur, quod ipsa duo sidera de caelo radios usque ad terras emittant. Dianam autem vocatam quasi Duanam, quod luna et die et nocte appareat.*

Dianam quoque . . . emittant is directly from Augustine, *De civ. Dei* vii.16, and probably indirectly from Varro: *Dianamque germanam eius similiter lunam et viarum praesidem (unde et virginem volunt quod via nihil pariat), et ideo ambos sagittas habere quod ipsa duo sidera de caelo radios terras usque pertendant.* Diana was not the guardian of roads in general, and certainly her association with them had nothing to do with her virginity. As the goddess Trivia, counterpart of the Greek Hecate (see §57 below), she was the overseer of three-way crossroads, crossroads then as now being regarded as uncanny. See Varro, *L.L.* vii.16 (*ab eo dicta Trivia, quod in trivio ponitur fere in oppidis Graecis*). Isidore is cited in *TLL* as the earliest extant source of the derivation of *Diana* from *Duana;* this too may be from Varro. Actually, Diana was another "shining" deity whose name contains the root *djo-*, like *Iuppiter*, Zeύs, and perhaps *Ianus*, who is sometimes described as the male counterpart of Diana (but see W. F. Otto, *PW*, "Janus," and the commentary on §37 above).

57. *Ipsam et Lucinam adseverant, eo quod luceat. Eandem et Triviam, eo quod tribus fungatur figuris. De qua Vergilius (Aen. 4,511):*

> *Tria virginis ora Dianae,*
> *quia eadem Luna, eadem Diana, eadem*
> *Proserpina vocatur.*

Isidore may have gotten *ipsam et . . . luceat* ultimately from Varro, although the passage in Varro (*L.L.* v.69) that has to do with Lucina is discussing Juno Lucina, not Diana: *Quae ideo quoque videtur ab Latinis Iuno Lucina dicta vel quod est et Terra, ut physici dicunt, et lucet; . . .* However, there is abundant evidence that in antiquity both Juno and Diana were called Lucina in their capacity as birth goddess; Varro says that this is because *mensibus actis produxit in lucem.* (*Cf.* Donatus, *Andria* 473, "*Lucina*" *ab eo, quod in lucem producat.* Here Juno Lucina is said to be the daughter of Juno and identified with the Greek εἰλείθυια and the Latin *Nixi.*) For Diana as Lucina, see Servius, *Aen.* iv.511; Cicero, *De nat. deor.* ii.27.68; Catullus, *Carm.* xxxiv.13ff.; Horace, *Carm.* iii.22.1ff. and the notes in the Shorey edition. The story went that Diana, being the firstborn, assisted Latona at the birth of her twin brother Apollo, and so although she is a maiden goddess she was invoked by women in childbirth. The truth is more probably that she and Juno both were originally mother goddesses who assisted in the birth of all living things (Juno's name may come from the same Indo-European *djo-* root as Diana's, so that they may once have been the same, or aspects of the same, goddess. See the notes to Catullus, *Carm.* xxxiv, in the E. T. Merrill edition.) The ancients had various explanations for the name *Trivia*, of which Isidore's is one of the more sensible. For the threefold nature of Trivia, see Horace, *Carm.* iii.22.4, and Shorey's note; also the passage from Vergil cited by Isidore. The correct explanation of the name is given by Varro, *L.L.* vii.16 (*ab eo dicta Trivia, quod in trivio ponitur fere in oppidis Graecis*); as a matter of fact, Trivia was in charge of Italian crossroads, but she had a Greek counterpart, Hecate Triodotis, who performed a similar function in Greece. The passage from Vergil is probably quoted indirectly from Servius, *Aen.* iv.511, where the goddess's three aspects are listed as *Lunae, Dianae, Proserpinae.* Elsewhere (*Aen.* iii.73) Servius confuses the issue by identifying her threefold nature as *Diana, Iuno, Proserpina.* Arevalo thinks that *Aen.* iii.73 is Isidore's source and that *Iuno* is a corruption of *Luna.* I think that *Iuno* is the correct reading and that she is Juno Lucina, equivalent to Luna; *cf.* Varro, *L.L.* v.69 for the identification of Juno Lucina with the moon. In both passages above, Servius identified Proserpina unequivocally with Diana, which makes §60 below something of a puzzle; but the confusion is not original with Isidore.

58. *Sed cum Luna fingitur (Prudent. i con. Symm. 363):*

> *Sublustri splendet amictu.*
> *cum subcincta iacit calamos, Latonia virgo est:*
> *cum subnixa sedet solio, Plutonia coniux.*
> *Latonia autem Diana, eo quod Latonae fuerit filia.*

The quotation from Prudentius is probably direct, since Isidore does not cite him as his source. Prudentius' triad is Luna/Diana/Proserpina, which agrees with that of Servius, *Aen.* iv.511. *Latonia autem . . . filia* is probably Isidore's own explanation; he could have verified all the pertinent information on Diana's birth, including her mother's name, from Servius, *Aen.* iii.73.

59. *Cererem, id est terram, a creandis frugibus adserunt dictam, appellantes eam nominibus plurimis. Dicunt etiam eam et Opem, quod opere melior fiat terra:*

Cererem . . . dictam is from Augustine, *De civ. Dei* iv.10 (*eandem terram Cererem*) and Servius, *Georg.* i.7 (*Ceres a creando dicta*). The etymology is correct. For *appellantes eam nominibus plurimis,* compare Augustine, *De civ. Dei* iv.10 and vii.24; although this may be Isidore's own observation on the

proliferation of overlapping functions and identities of the pagan goddesses. *Dicunt etiam . . . terra* is from Varro by way of Augustine, *De civ. Dei* vii.24: "*Tellurem,*" inquit, "*putant esse Opem, quod opere fiat melior.*" Originally Ceres and Tellus were two distinct but associated goddesses, the one of growing plants, the other of the fields themselves (see Ovid, *Fasti* i.673–674; Wissowa, *PW*, "Ceres"); but their identities eventually merged, especially after Ceres was also identified with the Greek Demeter, whose name was thought to be a Doric form of Γῆ Μήτηρ, "Mother Earth." Ops was originally simply a personification of material wealth, including crops. Later she was associated with the Greek Rhea, wife of Kronos, rather than with Demeter; but Rhea too was an earth goddess, and so both she and Ops came to be identified with Terra, Tellus, Ceres, and the whole plethora of other earth goddesses (see Rohde, *PW*, "Ops"). *Ops* and *opus* share a common root; work and grain were clearly related in the Roman mind. Isidore offers a different, and correct, explanation of why the earth goddess is called Ops at *Origines* xiv.1.1: *haec et Ops dicta, eo quod opem fert frugibus.*

60. *Proserpinam, quod ex ea proserpiant fruges:*

This ingenious but incorrect derivation is from Varro, in Augustine, *De civ. Dei* vii.24: *Proserpina quod ex ea proserpant fruges.* *Proserpina* is really a Latinization of the Greek Περσεφόνη, and has nothing to do with creeping of any sort. Proserpina/Περσεφόνη is normally equated with Kore, the daughter of Ceres/Demeter, rather than with Ceres herself; but in this passage Augustine very emphatically includes her among the aspects of Tellus, and since he is quoting Varro directly, presumably Varro did too. Servius (*Aen.* iii.113) equates her with both Terra and Mater Deum. She was called both *Ceres inferna* and *Iuno inferna* (*cf.* Statius, *Theb.* v.156; Vergil, *Aen.* iv.138) and was apparently a fertility goddess in her own right, though she was worshiped with Ceres/Demeter (see H. J. Rose, *HGM*, p. 92).

61. *Vestam, quod herbis vel variis vestita sit rebus, vel a vi sua stando. Eandem et Tellurem et Matrem magnam fingunt, turritam cum tympano et gallo et strepitu cymbalorum. Matrem vocatam, quod plurima pariat; magnam, quod cibum gignat; almam, quia universa animalia fructibus suis alit. Est enim alimentorum nutrix terra.*

Vestam, quod . . . stando is an amalgamation of Varro, in Augustine, *De civ. Dei* vii.24 (*Vestam quod vestiatur herbis*), Servius, *Aen.* i.292 (*Vesta autem dicta . . . quod variis vestita sit rebus*), and Servius, *Aen.* ii.296 (*Vesta dea ignis, quae, ut supra diximus, terra est: quod in medio mundo librata vi sua stet et ignem intra se habeat; cf.* Ovid, *Fasti* vi.299). Actually, Vesta was not an earth goddess at all, although she was commonly thought to be one in antiquity, the analogy being drawn between her round temple with its central fire and the earth which is round and *ignem intra se habeat*. It is more likely that the round temple preserved the shape of the prehistoric huts of the earliest Roman settlement, and that Vesta herself, as Ovid points out (*Fasti* vi.291, 297), was the sacred fire of the hearth, around which all the concerns of the household were centered (*cf.* Cicero, *De nat. deor.* ii.27.67; also Frazer's commentary on Ovid's *Fasti*, Vol. IV, pp. 181–186). She corresponds to the Greek Hestia; both names are descended from an Indo-European root akin to Sanskrit *vas*, "to burn." *Eandem et . . . fingunt* is from Varro, in Augustine, *De civ. Dei* vii.24 (*Nam et ipse Varro . . . unam deam vult esse Tellurem.* "*Eandem,*" *inquit*, "*dicunt Martrem Magnam, . . .*" *Cf.* Augustine, *De civ. Dei* iv.10; vii.16); the rest of the sentence is probably from the same passage, in which Augustine lists the attributes of the Great Mother: *tympanum, turres, Galli iactaio insana membrorum, crepitus cymbalorum, confictio leonum. Matrem vocatam, . . . gignat* is likewise from *De civ. Dei* vii.24 (*Matrem quod plurima pariat; Magnam quod cibum pariat*). *Almam, quia . . . alit*, however, is probably from Servius, *Aen.* i.306: *ALMA. alma lux dicta quod alat universa, unde et alma Ceres, quod nos alat.* (*Cf.* also *Aen.* x.252, *ALMA PARENS IDAEA DEUM. alma proprie est tellus ab eo quod nos alat*, and *Georg.* i.7.) The etymology for *alma* is correct. The Magna Mater was otherwise Cybele, the great eastern fertility goddess imported to Rome at the end of the Second Punic War. She was identified by the Greeks and Romans with a number of their native goddesses, including Demeter/Ceres, Terra (Tellus), and Rhea/Ops. *Est enim . . . terra* appears to be Isidore's comment. He was aware of the derivation of *alimentum* from *alo*; see *Origines* xx.2.2.

62. *Quod simulacrum eius cum clavi finguntur, quia tellus hieme clauditur, vere aperitur ut fruges nascantur. Quod tympanum habet, significare volunt orbem terrae.*

Quod simulacrum . . . aperitur is from Servius, *Aen.* x.252: *unde et simulacrum eius cum clavi pingitur, nam terra aperitur verno, hiemali clauditur tempore.* Isidore inserted *ut fruges nascantur*. The key was normally an attribute of underworld deities such as Hecate or Persephone, whose function it was to keep the shades confined to the realm of the dead. But other gods and goddesses were also sometimes depicted with a key, especially if mysteries were celebrated in their honor; among these was Cybele (see Hug, *PW*, "Schlussel"). *Quod tympanum . . . terrae* is from Augustine, *De civ. Dei* vii.24, quoting Varro (*quod tympanum habeat, significari esse orbem terrae*). The symbolic significance

attached by Varro, Servius, and other commentators to the goddess's drum (and indeed to all her attributes) is often ingenious but quite mistaken. The drum and other musical instruments associated with Cybele were used to arouse her devotees to orgiastic frenzy.

63. *Quod curru vehi dicitur, quia ipsa est terra quae pendet in aere. Quod sustinetur rotis, quia mundus rotatur et volubilis est. Quod leones illi subiciunt mansuetos, ut ostendant nullum genus esse tam ferum quod non subigi possit aut superari ab ea.*

Isidore took the goddess's chariot from Servius, *Aen.* iii.113: *ideo autem mater deum curru vehi dicitur, quia ipsa est terra, quae pendet in aëre: ideo sustinetur rotis, quia mundus rotatur et volubilis est.* The goddess was in fact conveyed in a wagon on her festival day, March 27, to the brook called the Almo, where a ceremonial *lavatio* was performed; an interesting parallel is the progress and bathing of the Teutonic goddess Nerthus, described by Tacitus, *Germania* 40. *Quod leones . . . ab ea* is a conflation of *Aen.* iii.113 (*ideo ei subiungantur leones ut ostendatur maternam pietatem totum posse superare*) and Varro, quoted by Augustine, *De civ. Dei* vii.24 (*Leonem, inquit, adiungunt solutum ac mansuetum, ut ostendant nullum genus esse terrae tam remotum ac vehementer ferum quod non subigi colique conveniat*). The idea that the lions symbolized the mastery of wild things by the goddess was popular in antiquity and perhaps right; but they were more commonly regarded as savage beasts whose depredations the goddess warded off, than as a symbol of uncultivated land rendered fruitful by her influence (see Schwenn, *PW*, "Kybele"; Frazer's commentary on Ovid's *Fasti*, Vol. III, pp. 216–217).

64. *Quod in capite turritam gestat coronam, ostendit superpositas terrae civitates quasi insignitas turribus constare. Quod sedes finguntur circa eam, quia cum omnia moveantur, ipsam non moveri.*

Quod in capite . . . constare is from Servius, *Aen.* iii.113: *quod autem turritam gestat coronam, ostendit superpositas terrae esse civitates, quas insignitas turribus constat.* There is no satisfactory explanation for Cybele's mural crown, which was usually worn by the personification of a city. Servius' interpretation may be correct, though Schwenn (*PW*, "Kybele") suggests that the crown may represent the role of her cult in the development of cities in her native Phrygia. *Quod sedes . . . moveri* is from Augustine, *De civ. Dei* vii.24: *quod sedens fingatur, circa eam cum omnia moveantur, ipsam non moveri.* The goddess was often depicted both sitting and enthroned, but the throne signified only majesty; the symbolic throne appears to be Isidore's creation, for he (or perhaps a later copyist) has written *sedes* for *sedens* and changed the verb from singular to plural. The shift of *circa eam* from *moveantur* to *finguntur*, however, may be the result of modern punctuation; both Arevalo and Lindsay punctuate the sentence with a comma after *eam*, indicating that neither of them closely examined the source of this particular passage.

65. *Quod Corybantes eius ministri cum strictis gladiis esse finguntur, ut significetur omnes pro terra sua debere pugnare. Quod gallos huic deae ut servirent fecerunt, significant qui semine indigeant, terram sequi oportere; in ea quippe omnia reperire.*

Isidore took his information on the Corybantes from Servius, *Aen.* iii.113: *ideo Corybantes eius ministri cum strictis gladiis esse finguntur, ut significetur omnes pro terra sua debere pugnare.* Actually, the Corybantes used their weapons to gash their limbs at the height of their frenzied dance in mourning for the annual death of the vegetation god Attis, the consort of Cybele. The blood, like the severed testicles of the Galli, may have been regarded as stimulating the productivity of the earth and the growth of vegetation. *Quod gallos . . . reperire* is from Varro, in Augustine, *De civ. Dei* vii.24 (*Quod Gallos huic deae ut servirent fecerunt, significat qui semine indigeant terram sequi oportere; in ea quippe omnia reperire*); Varro is quite mistaken. The purpose of the eunuch priests' self-mutilation was either to increase the fertility of the earth or to become one with the goddess by converting themselves to women (see Schwenn, *PW*, "Kybele"; Frazer's commentary to Ovid's *Fasti*, Vol. III, pp. 217–224, 244).

66. *Quod se apud eam iactant, praecipitur, inquiunt, ut qui terram colunt ne sedeant; semper enim esse quod agant. Cymbalorum autem aereorum sonitus, ferramentorum crepitus in colendo agro: sed ideo aere, quod terram antiqui aere colebant, priusquam ferum esset inventum.*

This entire section is from Augustine, *De civ. dei* vii.24, quoting Varro:

Quod se apud eam iactant, praecipitur, inquit, qui terram colunt ne sedeant; semper enim esse quod agant. Cymbalorum sonitus ferramentorum iactandorum ac manuum ⟨motum⟩ et eius rei crepitum in colendo agro qui fit significant; ideo aere, quod eam antiqui colebant aere, antequam ferrum esset inventum.

Isidore deleted *iactandorum ac manuum ⟨motum⟩ et eius rei . . . qui fit significant;* either he felt it was unnecessary, or he was puzzled as to what it had to do with the *cymbalorum sonitus.* The significance attached to the bronze is wrong (cymbals were normally made of bronze), but not without some basis in Roman religious practice: Bronze implements were prescribed for a number of religious observances, probably because the rituals dated from a time before

iron was in general use. For examples, see Macrobius, *Sat.* v.19.9ff.

67. *Eandem Vestam et ignem esse perhibent, quia terram ignem habere non dubium est, ut ex Aetna Vulcanoque datur intellegi. Et ideo virginem putant, quia ignis inviolabile sit elementum, nihilque nasci possit ex eo, quippe qui omnia quae arripuerit absumat.*

Isidore took *eandem Vestam . . . perhibent* from Augustine, *De civ. Dei* iv.10 (*Eandem terram Cererem, eandem etiam Vestam volunt, cum tamen saepius Vestam non nisi ignem esse perhibeant pertinentem ad focos*) and *quia terram . . . intellegi* from Servius, *Aen.* i.292 (*ipsa enim esse dicitur terra, quam ignem habere non dubium est, ut ex Aetna Vulcanoque et aliis locis ardentibus datur intellegi*). He is still pursuing the idea of Vesta as the fire under the earth, and omits Augustine's alternative explanation that she is the goddess of the domestic hearth-fire, which is correct (see commentary to §61 above). The remainder of the section is from Lactantius, *Inst. div.* i.12.5: *idcirco enim virginem putant Vestam, quia ignis inviolabile sit elementum nihilque nasci possit ex eo, quippe qui omnia quae arripuerit absumat.* For the association of unproductivity with virgin goddesses, compare Diana, §56 above.

68. *Ovidius in Fastis (6,291):*
> *Nec tu aliud Vestam quam vivam intellege flammam;*
> *nataque de flamma corpora nulla vides.*
Propterea et virgines ei servire dicuntur, eo quod scut ex virgine, ita nihil ex igne nascatur.

Lactantius continues (*Inst. div.* i.12.6) with a quotation from Ovid (*Ovidius in Fastis: nec tu aliud Vestam quam vivam intellege flammam/nataque de flamma corpora nulla vides*), which Isidore extracts. The remainder of the section is from Augustine, *De civ. Dei* iv.40 (*et ideo illi virgines solere servire quod sicut ex virgine, ita nihil ex igne nascatur*), and reiterates the symbolic connection between the sterility of fire and the unproductivity of the virgin goddess and her priestesses. Other authors (among them Ovid, *Fasti* vi.289–290; *cf.* also Dionysius of Halicarnassus, *Ant. Rom.* ii.66.2; Plutarch, *Numa* ix.5–7) consider that fire, as the purest of elements, should be served by undefiled priestesses. This latter theory may have some truth to it. The most convincing modern explanation regarding the origin of the cult of Vesta and the Vestals is that the sacred fire was once the hearth-fire of the Roman king, which represented the hearth of the community as a whole. The royal hearth, like those of private dwellings, was tended by the unmarried daughters of the household; thus the Vestals were originally the daughters of the king, whose authority over them passed in Republican times to the Pontifex Maximus. W. W. Fowler (*Roman Festivals*, pp. 148–149) and H. J. Rose (*Ancient Roman*

Religion, pp. 53–54) think that the Vestals were virgins because they assumed the symbolic duties of unmarried girls, but it may be, as J. G. Frazer argues (commentary to Ovid's *Fasti*, Vol. IV, pp. 204ff.), that the Romans, like many other peoples, regarded virgins (or abstinent people generally) as having special spiritual or magical force; this may be the reason why the maiden daughters of the household were entrusted with the care of the hearth and storeroom (for chastity in connection with the latter, see Columella, *De re rust.* xii.4.2ff.), and virgin priestesses with the hearth of the Roman state.

69. *Iunonem dicunt quasi ianonem, id est ianuam, pro purgationibus feminarum, eo quod quasi portas matrum natorum pandat, et nubentium maritis. Sed hoc philosophi. Poetae autem Iunonem Iovis adserunt sororem et coniugem: ignem enim et aerem Iovem, aquam et terram Iunonem interpretantur; quorum duorum permixtione universa gignuntur.*

Forcellini traces the etymology of *Iuno* from *ianua* no further than Isidore; it is, as he observes, absurd. Servius also connects the goddess with doors (*Aen.* ii.610; vii.610). The association apparently stems from her function as the birth goddess, Juno Lucina (see §57 above). *Pro purgationibus feminarum* is from Augustine, *De civ. Dei* vii.3 (*omnium purgandorum et pariendorum Iunonem et ideo eam non deesse purgationibus feminarum et partubus hominum*). The etymology from *ianua* may be from Varro; at *L.L.* v.67, he derives *Iuno* from *iuvat una*, but he is given to multiple etymologies. Modern scholars are not much more helpful than the ancients, and the actual derivation of her name is still in doubt. Forcellini postulates that it is a contraction of a feminine form *Iovina*, corresponding to masculine *Iovis*, both from the Indo-European *djo-* root, "shining." Haug, however, points out (*PW*, "Juno") that even in the earliest inscriptions the name was never spelled with an initial *d-*; he suggests that it comes from the same root as *iuvenis* and means "youthful"—i.e., she was originally the goddess of women of childbearing age, which is appropriate for the birth goddess Juno Lucina. Juno is referred to as *soror et coniunx* of Jupiter so often that the expression becomes almost an epithet. The best-known example is in Vergil, *Aen.* i.47 (*et soror et coniunx*); Servius comments on the line, and incidentally includes the phrase as his rubric, which is probably Isidore's source. *Cf.* also Cicero, *De nat. deor.* ii.26.66; Lactantius, *Inst. div.* i.10.14; Augustine, *De civ. Dei.* i.4; iv.10. The source of *ignem enim . . . gignuntur* appears to be Servius, *Georg.* ii.325 (*aliquotiens et pro aere et pro aethere Iuppiter, Iuno vero pro terra et aqua: sicut hoc loco intellegimus; nam aether non habet pluvias. unde Aetherem pro Iove accipimus, cui tribuuntur aer et aether: quae duo mixta terrae et umori universa procreant*), although

Isidore paraphrases the passage more freely than he usually does with Servius. The association of Juno with water and earth is somewhat unusual, although Varro (*L.L.* v.65, 67) identifies her with the earth. She is more often said to be the air (*cf.* Cicero, *De nat. deor.* ii.26.66), because of a supposed similarity between the word ἀήρ and the name of her Greek counterpart Ἥρα (Isidore himself mentions this in §98 below).

70. *Et sororem dicunt quod mundi pars est; coniugem, quod commixta concordat. Unde et Vergilius (Georg. 2,235):*

> *Tum pater omnipotens fecundis imbribus aether*
> *coniugis in gremium descendit.*

Et sororem . . . concordat may be Isidore's interpretation of the elements embodied in Jupiter and Juno. Lactantius (*Inst. div.* 1.5.19) and Augustine (*De civ. Dei* iv.10) both quote the passage from Vergil; Isidore may have taken it either from one of them or directly from the *Georgics*. In either case, he misquotes it; the second line should read *coniugis in gremium laetae discendit*.

71. *Minerva apud Graecos* Ἀθήνη *dicitur, id est, femina. Apud Latinos autem Minervam vocatam quasi deam et munus artium variarum. Hanc enim inventricem multorum ingeniorum perhibent, et inde eam artem et rationem interpretantur, quia sine ratione nihil potest contineri.*

Minerva apud . . . dicitur is from Augustine, *De civ. Dei* xviii.9 (*Minerva . . . quae Graece* Ἀθηνᾶ *dicitur*), but Isidore's translation of Ἀθήνη is his own, apparently the misunderstanding of an etymology which was current among the Greeks and is mentioned by Eustathius: Ἀθήνη, so they said, was from Ἀθήλη, because the goddess sprang full-grown from the head of her father Zeus and so had no need for the offices of a wet nurse (θηλή, "breast," "nipple," or θῆλυς, "female"). Arevalo also mentions the derivation from θῆλυς, but he takes it to mean *sine femina*, that is ἀμητώρ. Actually the name *Athene* is probably of prehellenic origin. In the following sentence, Isidore derives *Minerva* from the first syllables of *munus artium variarum*, a fine example of *compositio* that may be his own creation. *Hanc enim . . . perhibent* is from Augustine, *De civ. Dei* xviii.8: *multorum sane operum inventrix*. There is no extant source for the rest of the section, although the information is quite correct. Minerva, like Athena, was the goddess of the human intellect; her name comes from the root *men-* that is also found in *mens, memini*, and *moneo*. Isidore speaks of her as the *inventrix* of many arts again at *Origines* xv.1.44 and mentions that she was supposed to have invented weaving and the cultivation of the olive at *Origines* xix.20.1–2.

72. *Quae ratio, quia ex solo animo nascitur, animumque putant esse in capite et cerebro, ideo eam dicunt de capite Iovis esse natam, quia sensus sapientis, qui invenit omnia, in capite est.*

This section appears to be a continuation of whatever source Isidore is quoting in §71. There are numerous references, beginning with the twenty-eighth *Homeric Hymn*, to the birth of Athena from the head of Zeus, but the symbolic interpretation of it points to a fairly late theologian. *Dicunt de capite Iovis natam* resembles Servius, *Ecl.* ii.61 (*ideo dea artium Minerva dicitur quod de capite Iovis nata est*), which is the source of a similar passage at *Origines* xix.20.2, and Augustine, *De civ. Dei* xviii.8 (*quod enim de capite Iovis canitur, poetis et fabulis, non historiae rebusque gestis est applicandum*).

73. *In cuius pectore ideo caput Gorgonis fingitur, quod illic est omnis prudentia, quae confundit alios, et inperitos ac saxeos conprobat: quod et in antiquis Imperatorum statuis cernimus in medio pectore loricae, propter insinuandam sapientiam et virtutem.*

This section is largely compounded of two passages in Servius, *Aen.* viii.435 (*AEGIDAQUE HORRIFERAM. aegis proprie est munimentum pectoris aereum, habens in medio gorgonis caput: quod munimentum si in pectore numinis fuerit aegis vocatur: si in pectore hominis sicut in antiquis imperatorum statuis videmus, lorica dicitur*) and viii.438 (*hoc autem caput Minerva fingitur habere in pectore, quod illic est omnis prudentia, quae confundit alios et imperitos ac saxeos conprobat*). Isidore (or perhaps an intermediate scholiast) has combined the two rather freely, taking *caput Gorgonis* from the first and inserting it into the second, then returning to the first for the *loricae* of the emperors. Servius says nothing about a Gorgon's head on the latter. Isidore may have thought that there was supposed to be one because the *lorica* was the mortal warrior's equivalent of the aegis, or he may have had a particular piece of statuary in mind; such representations were not uncommon. He probably inserted *insinuandam . . . virtutem* himself. Actually, the Gorgon's head was originally an apotropaic charm intended to rout the enemy by its hideous appearance and/or by some magical virtue; the myth of the slaying of Medusa appears to have been invented to explain the device (H. J. Rose, *HGM*, pp. 29–30).

74. *Haec Minerva et Tritonia dicitur. Triton enim Africae palus est, circa quam fertur virginali apparuisse aetate, propter quod Tritonia nuncupata est. Unde et tanto proclivius dea credita, quanto minus origo eius innotuit.*

Haec Minerva . . . dicitur is probably Isidore's introduction to what follows. *Triton enim Africae palus est* is extracted from either Servius, *Aen.* ii.171

(*aut a Tritonide palude Africae*) or as Mommsen thinks, Solinus, *Coll. rerum memor.* xxvii.43 (*A Philaenorum aris non procul palus est quam Triton amnis influit*). The remainder of the section is from Augustine, *De civ. Dei* xviii.8 (*nam temporibus Ogygi ad lacum qui Tritonis dicitur, virginali apparuisse fertur aetate, unde et Tritonia nuncupata est; multorum sane operum inventrix et tanto proclivius dea credita quanto minus origo eius innotuit.* Cf. also Eusebius/Jerome, *Chron.* An. ccxxxix). There were several other rivers, springs, or other bodies of water, located for the most part in Greece, which were also named Tritonis or Triton, which claimed the distinction of being Athena's birthplace. This is probably not the origin of her name Tritonia (or Tritogeneia, as it often appears); see Kruse, *PW*, "Tritogeneia." The most that can be said of it is that its similarity to the name of the sea god Triton and to that of the various bodies of water suggests that in prehellenic times Athena may have had some connection with water.

75. *Pallas autem dicta vel ab insula Pallene in Thracia, in qua nutrita est; vel ἀπὸ τοῦ πάλλειν τὸ δόρυ, id est ab hastae concussione; vel quod Pallantem gigantem occiderit.*

The source of *Pallas autem . . . nutrita est* is obscure, but it may have a connection to Servius, *Georg.* iv.390, where Pallene is also said to be an island (actually it is a peninsula): *Pallene insula secundum Thermodontem dicta a Pallene, Sithonis filiae:* . . . The rest of the section is from Servius, *Aen.* i.39: *PALLASNE. Minerva ἀπὸ τοῦ πάλλειν τὸ δόρυ id est, a hastae concussione; vel quod Pallantem gigantem occiderit.* There may be some actual connection between πάλλειν and Pallas; Windberg (*PW*, "Pallas") speculates that the Titan or Giant Pallas (genitive Παλλάντος) was originally a prehellenic earth or earthquake god with whose cult Athena was associated. But it is more likely that Athena's title Pallas (genitive Παλλάδος) was related to παλλάξ, παλλακίς and simply meant "young woman" or "maiden" (=Parthenos). Compare the name *Iuno,* §69 above.

76. *Venerem exinde dicunt nuncupatam, quod sine vi femina virgo esse non desinat. Hanc Graeci Ἀφροδίτην vocant propter spumam sanguinis generantem. Ἀφρὸς enim Graece spuma vocatur.*

Venerem exinde . . . desinat is from Augustine, *De civ. Dei* vi.9, quoted from Varro: *Numquid Venus sola parum esset, quae ab hoc etiam dicitur nuncupata, quod sine vi femina virgo esse non desinat.* (Actually her name is related to *veneror* and *venustas;* Varro went out of his way to find an obscure etymology for it.) The rest of the section may come at least in part from Servius, *Aen.* v.801:

Venerem dicit a mare procreatam. et ut fert fabula, Caelus pater fuit Saturni. cui cum iratus filius falce virilia amputavit, delapsa in mare sunt: de quorum cruore et maris spuma nata dicitur Venus: unde et Ἀφροδίτη dicitur, ἀπὸ τοῦ ἀφροῦ.

This is assuming that Isidore knew enough Greek to convert genitive ἀφροῦ to nominative ἀφρός; it is possible, however, that he was drawing upon an intermediate scholiast. For Venus' birth from *spuma*, cf. Ovid, *Fasti* iv.62. Many attempts have been made by modern scholars to derive the name *Aphrodite* from various Indo-European and Semitic roots; none has been conclusive (see Dummler, *PW*, "Aphrodite"), and most lexicons fall back in desperation on the Hesiodic etymology (*Theog.* 196ff.) which Isidore gives here, which has at least the authority of great age. The specific reference to a "foam of blood" goes back to the medical writers of antiquity; see the commentary on the following section.

77. *Quod autem fingunt Saturnum Caelo patri genitalia abscidisse, et sanguinem fluxisse in mare, atque eo spuma maris concreta Venus nata est, illud aiunt quod per coitum salsi humoris substantia est; et inde* Ἀφροδίτην *Venerem dici, quod coitus spuma est sanguinis, quae ex suco viscerum liquido salsoque constat.*

Isidore may have gone to Lactantius, *Inst. div.* i.12.2, for *quod autem . . . abscidisse: verum etiam in patrem, cuius dicitur abscidisse genitalia;* his source for *Venus nata est* and *inde* Ἀφροδίτην *Venerem dici* is probably Servius, *Aen.* v.801 (see commentary, §76). Cf. Macrobius, *Sat.* i.8.6, for a similar account. Isidore's preoccupation with a physiological interpretation of the myth suggests that he may have been drawing upon one or more of the ancient medical writers; although he may be drawing upon Varro, whom Lactantius cites many times as one of the sources for his own physiological work *De opificio Dei.* The theory that semen is formed from blood is to be found in Galen, whom Isidore probably read in a Latin translation (*De usu part. corp. hum.* xvi.10: γένεσις μὲν γὰρ ἐξ αἵματός ἐστιν ἀκριβῶς πεπεμένου καὶ γάλακτι καὶ σπέρματι: *Lac enim et semen ex sanguine exacte cocto generantur*). Galen also observes, with reference to Aristotle (*De semine* i.5) that it is frothy because it is full of bubbles of air, and he makes mention of the birth of Venus from it. That it is actually a "foam of blood" (cf. *Origines* ix.6.4, where Isidore compares it to the froth on wine shaken in a cup) goes back to Diogenes of Apollonia, who is referred to in a fragment of Vendicianus Afer (Wellman, *Fr. d. gr. Ärzte* i.208.2): *semen . . . quod ⟨non⟩ est aliud quam spuma sanguinis spiritu collisi.* Isidore seems to have confused the act (*coitus*) with the substance it generates. His *salsus humor*, which he equates with the sea water from which the *spuma* is formed, must be the *tenuis liquor* mentioned in *Origines* xi.1.97 (cf. xi.1.104), which is distilled

from the blood. He may also have had in mind the passage from Servius, *Aen.* v.801, which explains that Venus is said to have been born from the sea *quia dicunt physici sudorem salsum esse, quem semper elicit coitus.*

78. *Ideo autem Venerem Vulcani dicunt uxorem, quia Venerium officium nonnisi calore consistit, unde est* (*Virg. Georg.* 3,97):

        Frigidus in Venerem senior.

This section appears to be a conflation of Servius, *Aen.* viii.373 (*constat enim a principio Venerem uxorem fuisse Vulcani*) and *Aen.* viii.389 (*namque ideo Vulcanus maritus fingitur Veneris, quod Venerium officium non nisi calore consistit, unde est frigidus in Venerem senior*). *Frigidus in Venerem senior*, as Lindsay has noted, is originally from Vergil, *Georg.* iii.97.

79. *Nam quod Saturnus dicitur patri Caelo virilia amputasse, quae in mare cadentia Venerem creaverunt, quod ideo fingitur quia nisi humor de caelo in terram descenderit, nihil creatur.*

This entire section is quoted from Servius, *Georg.* ii.406:

ET CURVO SATURNI DENTE. Id est falce, quae est in eius tutela. nam Saturnus dicitur patri Caelo virilia falce amputasse, quae in mare cadentia Venerem creaverunt: quod ideo fingitur, quia nisi umor de caelo in terras descenderit, nihil creatur.

Isidore omits all reference to the scythe, his concern here being with the symbolic descent of vitalizing moisture to earth.

80. *Cupidinem vocatum ferunt propter amorem. Est enim daemon fornicationis. Qui ideo alatus pingitur, quia nihil amantibus levius, nihil mutabilius invenitur. Puer pingitur, quia stultus est et inrationabilis amor. Sagittam et facem tenere fingitur. Sagittam, quia amor cor vulnerat; facem, quia inflammat.*

The Cupid or Amor whom the Romans knew was the naughty Hellenistic godlet who had replaced Hesiod's primal Eros (*Theog.* 120ff.). The Romans do not seem to have taken him very seriously, and he (or multiples of him) was often little more than a decorative accompaniment for Venus (see any number of Pompeian wall paintings). Isidore likewise relegates him to a single section in the wake of his mother. Apparently he was not familiar with Apuleius' account of the myth of Cupid and Psyche (*Met.* iv.300ff.), which presents Cupid in a more mature but equally pretty role. This section is a rather free paraphrase and amalgamation of passages in Servius (or a later scholiast who drew upon him) and Augustine. *Cupidinem vocatum . . . . amorem* is from *Aen.* i.663 (*Cupidinem vocant hoc quod facit "amorem").* The charge that he is god of fornication sounds ecclesiastical; Vat. Myth. ii.35 more charitably calls him *amoris deum. Qui ideo . . . invenitur* is also from *Aen.* i.663 (*alatus autem ideo est, quia amantibus nec levius aliquid nec mutabilius invenitur); puer pingitur . . . amor* likewise (*nam quia turpidinis est stulta cupiditas puer pingitur*), with the reference to *turpitudo* deleted and the one to irrationality added from Augustine, *Contra Faust.* xx.9 (*et Cupidinem puerum volitantem ac sagittantem, quod irrationabilis et instabilis amor corda vulnerat miserorum*). Note that Augustine considers only *irrationabilis et instabilis amor* to be harmful, while Isidore regards *amor* generally as *stultus et irrationabilis.* The rest of the section is a conflation of the passage from Augustine, *Contra Faust.* above, and Servius, *Aen.* iv.1: *et bene adludit ad Cupidinis tela, ut paulo post ad faculam, ut "et caeco carpitur igni": nam sagittarum vulnus est, facis incendium.*

81. *Pan dicunt Graeci, Latini Silvanum, deum rusticorum, quem in naturae similitudinem formaverunt; unde et Pan dictus est, id est omne. Fingunt enim eum ex universali elementorum specie.*

It is hard to say why Isidore equates Pan with the Italian Silvanus, unless it is because, as Servius says (Aen. viii.601), people regarded the latter as well as the former as *pecorum et agrorum deum.* To Vergil's mind they were two separate gods (*Ecl.* x.24; *Georg.* ii.494), and Vat. Myth. iii.8.2 says as much (though the fact that he felt obliged to do so indicates that a certain amount of confusion did exist). Apart from this puzzling insertion, *Pan dicunt . . . omne* is from Servius, *Ecl.* ii.31: *nam Pan deus est rusticus in naturae similitudinem formatus, unde et pan dictus, id est omne.* The derivation itself is from Varro; *cf.* Vat. Myth. iii.8.2. *Fingunt enim . . . specie* may be Isidore's own introduction to what follows. The view that Pan was the god of all nature was a late one based on the false etymology of his name from πᾶν; the name actually comes from the Indo-European root *pa-* (as in Latin *pasco, pastor*) which means "to feed, pasture." Pan was the god of herds and flocks; hence his goatish appearance and shepherd's pipes.

82. *Habet enim cornua in similitudinem radiorum solis et lunae. Distinctam maculis habet pellem, propter caeli sidera. Rubet eius facies ad similitudinem aetheris. Fistulam septem calamorum gestat, propter harmoniam caeli, in qua septem sunt soni et septem discrimina vocum.*

The whole of this section, with the exception of *distinctam maculis . . . sidera,* is from Servius, *Ecl.* ii.31:

habet enim cornua in radiorum solis et cornuum lunae similitudinem: rubet eius facies ad aetheris imitationem;

in pectore nebridem habet stellatam ad stellarum imaginem; . . . fistulam septum calamorum habet, propter harmoniam caeli, in qua septem soni sunt, ut diximus in *Aeneide* (vi.646), septem discrimina vocum.

The precise origin of *distinctam maculis . . . sidera* is somewhat of a puzzle. Junius Philargyrius, a late Vergilian scholiast who drew upon both Servius and very probably Aelius Conatus' commentary on Vergil, contains the following (*Ecl.* ii.32, rec. I): *Pan, pastoralis Deus . . . significat . . . per pellem maculosam caeli sidera.* Cf. the even later *Brevis expositio in Verg. Georg.* i. 17: *pellis maculis distincta quae variam designat imaginem siderum.* It is possible that Isidore took the reference to Pan's spotted hide from Philargyrius, inserting it into the passage from Servius and adjusting the wording as necessary. It is also possible that Isidore took it from the same source that Philargyrius did, and that this source was Donatus. It is even possible that Isidore took the entire passage on Pan from Donatus, and that its similarity to the passage in Servius is explained by the fact that Servius took his information on Pan from Donatus, altering *distinctam maculis . . . sidera* to *in pectore . . . imaginem.*

83. *Villosus est, quia tellus convestita est +agitventibus+. Pars eius inferior foeda est, propter arbores et feras ut pecudes. Caprinas ungulas habet, ut soliditatem terrae ostendat, quem volunt rerum et totius naturae deum; unde Pan quasi omnia dicunt.*

The first sentence of this section contains a crux which Arevalo suggests should be emended to *agitata ventis.* Other commentators, dissatisfied with this, have proposed *vegetuntibus* (L. C. Purser, in his review of Lindsay's edition of the *Origines, Hermathena,* XXXVIII [1912], p. 188) and *gignentibus* (J. E. Sandys, "A Correction of Isidore, VIII.xi §83," *Classical Review,* 1915, pp. 139–140). Philargyrius, however, has the following (*Ecl.* ii.32, rec. I): *Villosus est, quia vestitis gaudet terra,* and on the basis of this I propose that *est +agitventibus+* should be emended to *gaudet vestibus.* Isidore may have inserted the *convestita* from Servius, *Aen.* i.292, in which Vesta (=Tellus) is spoken of as *variis vestita . . . rebus.* (An alternative emendation, which is less satisfactory but does less violence than Arevalo's to the extant letters, is to change *+agitventibus+* to *agri vestibus.*) *Pars eius . . . ostendat* has as its source Servius, *Ecl.* ii.31 (*pars eius inferior hispida est propter arbores, virgulta, feras; caprinos pedes habet, ut ostendat terrae soliditatem*). But even here there are problems. Why, for example, does Isidore have *foeda* instead of *hispida?* Perhaps, as was suggested in the preceding section, his source for Pan was Donatus rather than Servius and the reading in Donatus was *foeda.* Or he may simply have wanted to change *hispida* to a more emotionally colorful word. It is even possible, though less likely, that he was unfamiliar with the meaning of *hispida* and changed it to a word he understood. His text also contains *arbores et feras ut pecudes* for Servius' *arbores, virgulta, feras*. The change from *virgulta, feras* to *feras . . . pecudes* is perplexing, but less so than the insertion of *ut* between them. As it stands, it means "wild animals (behaving) like flocks," which must be corrupt. The simplest emendation, which brings the passage into the closest agreement with Servius, is to change the *ut* to *et*; this has some manuscript support. Another possibility is that Isidore wrote *ut ferae et pecudes*, meaning that the trees make the earth shaggy, and therefore Pan is covered with hair like an animal; if the *et* and the *ut* were subsequently transposed, a sharp-eyed copyist might have changed *ferae* to *feras* to agree with *propter*. This would at least explain the inclusion of *pecudes*. *Quem volunt . . . dicunt* appears to be a recapitulation of the beginning of §81, from Servius, *Ecl.* ii.31.

84. *Isis lingua Aegyptiorum terra appellatur, quam Isin volunt esse. Fuit autem Isis regina Aegyptiorum, Inachis regis filia quae de Graecia veniens Aegyptios litteras docuit, et terras colere instituit; propter quod et terram eius nomine appellaverunt.*

Here begins a brief digression on the gods of Egypt. *Isis autem . . . esse* is from Servius, *Aen.* viii.696: *Isis autem lingua Aegyptiorum esse terra, quam Isin volunt esse.* The name is in fact Egyptian, although we know it in its Greek form, and Isis was an earth or fertility goddess whose consort was the dying and resurrecting vegetation god Osiris/Serapis (*cf.* Varro, *L.L.* v.57; Macrobius, *Sat.* i.21.11). Augustine (*De civ. Dei* xviii.37) says that she was the daughter of Inachus and also that she taught the use of writing to the Egyptians:

Quid autem sapientiae potuit esse in Aegypto, antequam eis Isis, quam mortuam tamquam magnam deam colendam putarunt, litteras traderet? Isis porro Inachi filia fuisse proditur, qui primus regnare coepit Argivis, quando Abrahae iam nepotes reperiuntur exorti.

This may be Isidore's source for *Fuit autem . . . instituit* (it is very probably the source for *Origines* i.3.5), but Isidore may also have been drawing upon two other passages in *De civ. Dei*, xviii.3

Nam et Io filia Ianchi fuisse perhibetur, quae postea Isis appellata ut magna dea culta est in Aegypto; . . . et quod late iusteque imperaverit eisque multa commoda et litteras instituerit, hunc honorem illi habitum esse divinum, . . .

and xviii. 39

Neque enim quisquam dicere audebit mirabilium disciplinarum eos peritissimos fuisse, antequam litteras nossent, id est, antequam Isis eo venisset easque ibi docuisset.

The legend goes back to Varro (see Augustine, *De civ. Dei* xviii.40), who may be Isidore's ultimate source for her teaching both the alphabet and agriculture. The goddess is identified with Argive Io by a number of authors; *cf.* Ovid, *Fasti* i.454; *Met.* i.747; Hyginus, *Fab.* cxlv; Lactantius, *Inst. div.* i.11.20. The reason for this is not far to seek: Isis was often depicted with either a cow's head or a goddess-crown adorned with cow's horns, generally with a sun-disc set between them, which the Greeks mistook for a moon-disc. The Ptolemies took advantage of this coincidental resemblance between Isis and Io to establish ties between the goddess whom they claimed as an ancestor and the Argive kings of the heroic period. *Cf.* Serapis in the following section.

85. *Serapis omnium maximus Aegyptiorum deus. Ipse est Apis rex Argivorum, qui navibus transvectus in Aegyptum, cum ibidem mortuus fuisset, Serapis appellatus est; propterea quia arca, in qua mortuus ponitur, quam sarcophagum vocant, σορὸς dicitur Graece, et ibi eum venerari sepultum coeperunt, priusquam templum eius esset instructum. Velut σορὸς et Apis, Sorapis primo, deinde una littera commutata Serapis dictus est.*

Isidore's information on Serapis is entirely from Augustine, *De civ. Dei* xviii.5, who in turn quotes it from Varro:

His temporibus rex Argivorum Apis navibus transvectus in Aegyptum, cum ibi mortuus fuisset, factus est Serapis omnium maximus Aegyptiorum deus. Nominis autem huius, cur non Apis etiam post mortem, sed Serapis appellatus sit, facillimam rationem Varro reddidit. Quia enim arca in qua mortuus ponitur, quod omnes iam sarcophagum vocant, σορὸς dicitur Graece, et ibi eum venerari sepultum coeperant, priusquam templum eius esset extructum, velut soros et Apis Sorapis primo, deinde una littera, ut fieri adsolet, commutata Serapis dictus est.

Isidore has deleted only the one sentence *Nominis autem . . . reddidit*, which he evidently regarded as unnecessary. It goes without saying that Serapis was never an Argive king; the etymology of his name from σορὸς is mistaken. It is most probably a contraction of Osiris-Apis, Isis' consort Osiris in his capacity of the lord of the dead. The connection with the kings of Argos reflects another attempt on the part of the Ptolemies to establish ancestors for themselves among the legendary heroes of Greece (*Cf.* Isis/Io, §84).

86. *Apis fuit apud Aegyptios taurus Serapi consecratus, et ab eo ita cognominatus, quem Aegyptus instar numinis colebat, eo quod de futuris daret quaedam manifesta signa. Apparebat enim in Menphis. Quem centum antistites prosequebantur et repente velut lymphatici praecanebant. Huius capitis imaginem sibi in eremo Iudaei fecerunt.*

Isidore's sources for Apis are uncertain. The most likely one for *Apis fuit . . . praecanebant* is Solinus, xxxii.17–20, although if this is Isidore's source, he has paraphrased it considerably:

Inter omnia quae Aegyptus habet digna memoratu, praecipue bovem mirantur: Apim vocant. hunc ad instar colunt numinis, insignem albae notae macula, . . . mox alter nec sine publico luctu requiritur, quem repertum centum antistes Memphim prosequuntur, ut incipiat ibi sacris initiatus sacer fieri. . . . dat omina manifestantia de futuris: . . . pueri Apim gregatim sequuntur et repente velut lymphatici praecinunt.

For Apis as the golden calf, see Lactantius, *Inst. div.* iv.10.12: *Cum enim Moyses dux eorum ascendisset in montem atque ibi quadraginta diebus moraretur, aureum caput bovis quem vocant Apim, quod eos in signo praecederet, figurarent.*

87. *Fauni a fando, vel ἀπὸ τῆς φωνῆς dicti, quod voce, non signis ostendere viderentur futura. In lucis enim consulebantur a paganis, et responsa illis non signis, sed vocibus dabant.*

Fauni a fando is originally from Varro; cf. *L.L.* vii.36: *hos versibus quos vocant Saturnios in silvestribus locis traditum est solitos fari, ⟨futura a⟩ quo fando Faunos dictos.* See also Servius, *Aen.* vii.47; viii.314, which may be taken from Varro. Servius, *Aen.* vii.81, provides the etymology ἀπὸ τῆς φωνῆς and the source for *et responsa . . . darent: FAUNI. Faunus* ἀπὸ τῆς φωνῆς *dictus, quod voce, non signis, ostendit futura.* There was considerable doubt, even in early times, as to whether Faunus was one deity or many forest spirits akin to the Greek Panes or Panites (Otto, *PW*, "Faunus"), but his (or their) prophetic nature is well-attested; cf. Varro and Servius, above, also Vergil, *Aen.* viii.81ff. *Faunus* probably does not come from either φωνή or *fando*, but from the root *fav-* as in *faveo*, and means "favorable" or "helpful." Cf. Macrobius, *Sat.* i.2.22; Servius, *Georg.* i.10.

88. *Genium autem dicunt, quod quasi vim habeat omnium rerum gignendarum, seu a gignendis liberis; unde et geniales lecti dicebantur a gentibus, qui novo marito sternebantur.*

Isidore's source for *Genium autem . . . gignendarum* is Varro, in Augustine, *De civ. Dei* vii.13: *Quid est genius? "Deus," inquit, "qui praepositus est ac vim habet omnium rerum gignendarum."* The etymology is correct; the Romans regarded one's Genius as the tutelary deity or ἀγαθὸς δαίμων, that helped one into life and thereafter watched over one and influenced one's life for the better. Women were thought to have a Juno instead of a Genius; unlike her male counterpart, Juno developed into a distinct deity in her own right, as the goddess of womanly concerns and particularly of childbirth (see §69, above). Places, buildings, and groups of people, as well as individuals, were believed to have a Genius. The marriage bed was sacred to the Genius of the household, who presumably looked after the begetting of children. Isidore's *seu a . . . sternebatur*, therefore, is correct; he takes it from Servius, *Aen.* vi.603: *GENIALIBUS. veluti genialibus: nam geniales proprie sunt qui sternuntur puellis nubentibus, dicti a generandis liberis.* Although the individual's Genius was worshiped privately as a sort of personal guardian angel, the Genius of the Roman people, and later that of the emperor, were worshiped publicly and were quite important. This may be why Augustine (*De civ. Dei* vii.2) includes Genius among his "select" gods. By Isidore's time, of course, neither public Genius was worshiped, and it may be that Isidore knew only of the individual Genius; hence his relegation to a position among the lesser and foreign gods at the end of the chapter.

89. *Haec et alia sunt gentilium fabulosa figmenta, quae interpretata sic habentur, ut ea non intellecta damnabiliter tamen adorent.*

This section, clearly Isidore's own editorializing, together with §29 (cf. *vanas fabulas* there with *fabulosa figmenta*) serves to bracket the discussion of the major and minor pagan gods. Hereafter, Isidore moves on to supernatural beings which are not properly considered gods, such as *fata*, nymphs, and *lamiae*.

90. *Fatum autem dicunt esse quidquid dii fantur, quidquid Iuppiter fatur. A fando fatum dicunt, id est a loquendo. Quod nisi hoc nomen iam in alia re soleret intellegi, quo corda hominum nolumus inclinare, rationabiliter possumus a fando fatum appellare.*

Fatum autem . . . fatur is taken from Servius, *Aen.* ii.77 (*fata sunt quae dii fantur;* cf. ii.54) and xii.808 (*sed Iuno sciens fatum esse quidquid Iupiter dixerit*). *A fando . . . loquendo* is from Augustine, *De civ. Dei* v.9 (probably quoted from Varro; cf. *L.L.* v.52): *nisi forte ut fatum a fando intellegamus, id est a loquendo.* The etymology is correct, though there was some question in antiquity (reflected by Servius and thence by Isidore) as to whether "Fate" represented the "speaking" of Jupiter alone, or of all the gods in general, or whether it was an independent agency or deity or group of deities in its own right (see Varro, *L.L.* vi.52; Otto, *PW*, "Fatum"). The remainder of the section is from the same passage in Augustine, *De civ. Dei* v.9 (*Hac itaque ratione possemus a fando fatum appellare nisi hoc nomen iam in alia re soleret intellegi quo corda hominum nolumus inclinare*), somewhat rearranged and with *hac ratione* changed to *rationabiliter* so that the passage would make sense when lifted out of context. As Augustine observes, the idea of Fate, in the sense of events preordained by God, was not incompatible with Christian doctrine; his objection is to the use of the word *fatum*, because of its pagan connotations.

91. *Non enim abnuere possumus esse scriptum in litteris sanctis (Psalm. 61,12): 'Semel locutus est Deus: duo haec audivi,' et cetera. Quod enim dictum est, 'semel locutus est,' intellegitur inmobiliter, hoc est incommutabiliter est locutus; sicut novit incommutabiliter omnia quae futura sunt, et quae ipse facturus est.*

Isidore continues to quote from Augustine's consideration of the Christian versus the pagan concept of fate, *De civ. Dei* v.9:

non enim abnuere possumus esse scriptum in litteris sanctis: Semel locutus est Deus, duo haec audivi, quoniam potestas Dei est, et tibi, Domine, misericordia qui reddis unicuique secundum opera eius. Quod enim dictum est: semel locutus est, intellegitur "inmobiliter," hoc est incommutabiliter, "est locutus," sicut novit incommutabiliter omnia quae futura sunt et quae ipse facturus est.

92. *Tria autem fata fingunt in colo et fuso digitisque filum ex lana torquentibus, propter tria tempora: praeteritum, quod in fuso iam netum atque involutum est: praesens, quod inter digitos neentis traicitur: futurum in lana quae colo inplicata est, et quod adhuc per digitos neentis ad fusum tamquam praesens ad praeteritum traiciendum est.*

The Parcae in their triple form probably represent the Latin assimilation of the Greek Μοῖραι, Parca (singular) having been originally an Italian birth goddess. Certainly the image of three goddesses who respectively spin, measure, and clip the thread of life is Greek. Isidore takes his information about them from Augustine, *Contra Faust.* xx.9:

et tria Fata in colo et fuso digitisque filum ex lana torquentibus, propter tria tempora, praeteritum quod in fuso iam netum atque involutum est, praesens quod inter digitos nentis traiicitur, futuram in lana, quae colo implicata est, quod adhuc per digitos nentis ad fusum, tanquam per praesens ad praeteritum traiiciendum est; . . .

Cf. Philargyrius, *Ecl.* iv.46; Lactantius, *Inst. div.* ii.10.19 on the three times; Apuleius, *De mun.* xxviii.373 on the symbolic interpretation of the Parcae.

93. *Parcas* κατ' ἀντίφρασιν *appellatas, quod minime parcant. Quas tres esse voluerunt: unam, quae vitam hominis ordiatur; alteram, quae contexat; tertiam, quae rumpat. Incipimus enim cum nascimur, sumus cum vivimus, desiimus cum interimus.*

Parcas κατ' ἀντίφρασιν . . . *parcant* is from Servius, *Aen.* i.22 (*et dictae sunt Parcae* κατ' ἀντίφρασιν*, quod nulli parcant*). *Cf.* Donatus, *Ars. gram.* iii.6. (The name is really from a root related to *plecto* or *plico*.)

The remainder of the section, on why it is necessary to have three goddesses, is from Lactantius, *Inst. div.* ii.10.20: *et incipimus enim, cum nascimur, et sumus, cum vivimus, et desinimus, cum interimus. unde etiam tres Parcas esse voluerunt: unam quae vitam hominis ordiatur, alteram quae contexat, tertiam quae rumpat ac finiat.*

94. *Fortunam a fortuitis nomen habere dicunt, quasi deam quandam res humanas variis casibus et fortuitis inludentem; unde et caecam appellant, eo quod passim in quoslibet incurrens sine ullo examine meritorum, et ad bonos et ad malos venit. Fatum autem a fortuna separant: et fortuna quasi sit in his quae fortuitu veniunt, nulla palam causa; fatum vero adpositum singulis et statutum aiunt.*

Fortuna was a much more popular goddess with the Romans than the Parcae were. Originally a goddess of increase, she came to be the goddess of chance (properly Fors Fortuna). Her name is in fact from the same root as *fortuitus* (cf. *De civ. Dei* iv.11) and *fors*, perhaps lengthened from *fors* in the same manner as *Neptunus* from *nubes*. Isidore took *fortunam . . . dicunt* from Augustine, *De civ. Dei* iv.18 (*Ubi est definitio illa Fortunae? Ubi est quod a fortuitis etiam nomen accepit?*), and he probably took it from Varro. *Quasi deam . . . inludentem* is from Lactantius, *Inst. div.* iii.28.6 (*non dissimili errore credunt esse fortunam quasi deam quandam res humanas variis casibus inludentem*), with *et fortuitis* inserted to demonstrate the connection between that word and the goddess's name. Isidore's remarks on her blind and random beneficence, *unde et . . . venit*, are compressed, in the interest of reducing a florid rhetorical passage to a simple statement, from Augustine, *De civ. Dei* iv.18:

fortuna vero quae dicitur bona sine ullo examine meritorum fortuito accidit hominibus et bonis et malis, unde etiam Fortunam nominatur. Quo modo ergo bona est, quae sine ullo iudicio venit ad bonos et ad malos? Ut quid autem colitur, quae ita caeca est passim in quoslibet incurrens ut suos cultores plerumque praetereat et suis contemptoribus haereat.

I find no direct source for Isidore's distinction between Fate and Fortune, though *et statutum aiunt* may come from Servius, *Ecl.* iv.47: *Et fixa sunt statuta fatorum.*

95. *Aiunt et tres Furias feminas crinitas serpentibus, propter tres affectus, quae in animis hominum multas perturbationes gignunt, et interdum cogunt ita delinquere, ut nec famae nec periculi sui respectum habere permittant. Ira, quae vindictam cupit: cupiditas, quae desiderat opes: libido, quae appetit voluptates. Quae ideo Furiae appellantur, quod stimulis suis mentem feriant et quietam esse non sinant.*

The identification of the three Furies with *ira*, *cupiditas*, and *libido* is from the *Epitome* to Lactantius, *Inst. div.*, 56.1:

Tres adfectus vel ut ita dicam tres Furiae sunt, quae in
animis hominum tantas perturbationes cient et interdum
cogunt ita delinquere ut nec famae nec periculi sui
respectum habere permittant, ira quae vindictam
cupit, avaritia quae desiderat opes, libido quae adpetit
voluptates.

This is the only point in *Origines* viii.11 in which
Isidore draws upon the *Epitome* rather than the
Institutiones proper. The snaky hair of the Furies
was well attested by several poets whom Isidore
would have known (*cf.* Vergil, *Aen.* vii.329; 346;
447–450); he may have inserted *crinitas serpentibus*
with no particular source in mind. The derivation
of *Furiae* from *ferio* may be from Varro; the true one,
from *furia* and *furo* (akin to Greek ϑοῦρος, ϑήρ and
Latin *fera* and *ferox*) is not so exotic.

96. *Nymphas deas aquarum putant, dictas a nubibus.*
Nam ex nubibus aquae, unde derivatum est. *Nymphas*
deas aquarum, quasi numina lympharum. *Ipsas*
autem dicunt et Musas quas et numphas, nec inmerito.
Nam aquae motus musicen efficit.

The source for this entire section and the one
following is Junius Philargyrius, *Ecl.* ii.46 (*Nymphas*
deas aquarum putant dictas a nubibus, nam ex nubibus
aquae. *Unde et derivatam est quasi numina aquarum*
vel lympharum. *Ipsas autem dicunt et Musas quas*
et Nymphas, nam aquae motus musicam efficit). The
etymology of νύμφη/*nympha* here is probably correct.
Although no one has arrived at a satisfactory derivation for the word, there appears to be some connection between it and the root of *nubes*, *nubo*, and
Greek νεφέλη; and as Heichelheim (*PW*, "Nymphai")
points out, deriving νύμφη from the custom of veiling a
bride puts too narrow a meaning on it. If Neptune
as a rain god is connected with clouds (see §58
above), there is no reason why nymphs, who were
in particular water spirits, should not also be. The
connection between *lympha* and *nympha*, which is
correct (except that *lympha* came from *nympha*
instead of *nympha* from the *compositio* of *numina*
and *lympharum*), goes back to Varro (see *L.L.*
vii.87, *lymphata dicta a lympha;* ⟨*lympha*⟩ *a nympha*).
The nymphs were even more emphatically water
goddesses among the Romans than they were among
the Greeks. That men were first inspired to make
music by the babbling of brooks is a pretty conceit,
but the connection between Muses, nymphs, and
water is more probably that the Muses were spirits of
certain sacred springs, the waters of which gave in-
spiration to those who drank of them.

97. *Nympharum apud gentiles varia sunt vocabula.*
Nymphas quippe montium Oreades dicunt, silvarum
Dryades, fontium Hamadryades, camporum Naides,
maris Nereides.

The source for this section, as noted above, is
Philargyrius, *Ecl.* ii.46 (*Nympharum apud gentiles*
varia sunt vocabula. *Nymphas quippe montium*
Oriades dicunt, sylvarum Dryades, fontium Hama-
dryades, camporum Meliades, maris Naides), because
Isidore inherited the error concerning the Hamadryades from him. Philargyrius miscopied from
his source (Donatus?). Servius, who in all likeli-
hood also drew upon Donatus (see E. K. Rand, "Is
Donatus' Commentary on Virgil Lost?" *Classical*
Quarterly **X** (1916): pp. 159–160) has the following
at *Aen.* i.500: *OREADES. nymphae montium Oreades*
dicuntur, silvarum Dryades, quae cum silvis nascuntur
Amadryades, fontium Napeae vel Naides, maris vero
Nereides. Philargyrius seems to have read *Hama-*
dryades with *fontium*, omitted *quae cum silvis*
nascuntur and *Napeae vel*, and taken *Naides* with
maris. Isidore compounds the confusion by himself
omitting *Meliades* from Philargyrius (Servius does
not include a reference to nymphs of the fields, which
makes me think that Philargyrius was working
directly from Donatus), and so converts the Naides
to field nymphs. He then seems to have taken
Nereides from Servius to go with *maris.*

98. *Heroas dicunt a Iunone traxisse nomen.* *Graece*
enim Iuno Ἥρα *appellatur.* *Et ideo nescio quis*
filius eius secundum Graecorum fabulam ἥρως *fuit*
nuncupatus; hoc videlicet velut mysticum significante
fabula, quod aer Iunoni deputetur, ubi volunt heroas
habitare. *Quo nomine appellant alicuius meriti ani-*
mas defunctorum, quasi ἀήρωας, *id est viros aerios et*
caelo dignos propter sapientiam et fortitudinem.

Isidore's source for *heroas dicunt . . . defunctorum*
is Augustine, *De civ. Dei* x.21:

Hoc enim nomen a Iunone dicitur tractum, quod Graece
Iuno Ἥρα appellatur, et ideo nescio quis filius eius
secundum Graecorum fabulas Heros fuerit nuncupatus,
hoc videlicet veluti mysticum significante fabula, quod
aer Iunoni deputetur, ubi volunt cum daemonibus heroas
habitare, quo nomine appellant alicuius meriti animas
defunctorum.

Isidore's elaboration upon this last statement, *quasi*
ἀήρωας, *. . . fortitudinem*, may have been drawn
from a scholiast now lost; ἀήρωας looks as if it is a
back formation from ἥρως, ἥρωος, an invention that
would have taxed Isidore's slender knowledge of
Greek. An actual connection seems to exist between
Ἥρα and ἥρως, though not the one given here;
neither word has any connection with ἀήρ. The
most reasonable explanation is that both Ἥρα and
ἥρως come from an Indo-European root *sar*, "guard-
ing," "protecting," which appears in Latin *servare*.
The heroes were originally the spirits of dead leaders
who were believed to watch over their people in
death as in life, and to whom shrines were erected
and offerings made.

99. *Penates gentiles dicebant omnes deos quos domi colebant. Et penates dicti, quod essent in penetralibus, id est in secretis. Hi dii quomodo vocabantur, vel quae nomina habuerint, ignoratur.*

Penates gentiles . . . colebant is from Servius, *Aen.* ii.514: *CONPLEXA PENATES. Penates sunt omnes dii qui domi coluntur.* For *et penates . . . secretis,* cf. Servius, *Aen.* ii.484, *PENETRALIA. Id est domorum secreta dicta penetralia aut ab eo quod est penitus, aut a penates.* Note that if this is Isidore's source, he has reversed the etymology. Actually, *penates* and *penetralia* share a common root *pa-*, "to feed"; see the commentary on Pan, §83 above. It is possible that Isidore got this information and that which follows it from Varro or an extract of Varro instead of from Servius; see Arnobius, *Adv. nat.* iii.40: *Varro qui sunt introrsus atque in intimis penetralibus caeli deos esse censet quos loquimur, nec eorum numerum nec nomina sciri.* The *penates* were the guardian spirits of the storeroom of the house, and they were probably not personified in early times; later, attempts were made to identify them with various of the major gods. See Servius, *Aen.* i.378 (Neptune and Apollo, Juno); ii.296 (Jupiter, Juno, Minerva); ii.325 (Ceres, Pales, Fortuna); iii.12 (Jupiter, Juno, Minerva, Mercury, or Castor and Pollux). Isidore's observation, *Hi dii . . . ignoratur,* seems justified.

100. *Manes deos mortuorum dicunt, quorum potestatem inter lunam et terram asserunt; a quibus et mane dictum existimant; quos putant ab aere, qui μανός, id est rarus est, manes dictos, sive quia late manant per auras, sive quia mites sunt, inmanibus contrarii, nomine hoc appellantur. Apuleius autem ait eos κατ' ἀντίφρασιν dici manes, hoc est mites ac modestos, cum sint terribiles et inmanes, ut Parcas, ut Eumenides.*

It is not clear what Isidore means by *deos mortuorum;* possibly the gods who rule the underworld, but more likely just the deified spirits of the dead, as in the formula *Dis Manibus,* followed by the name of the deceased in the genitive. If the latter, his source was probably Varro, in Augustine, *De civ. Dei* viii.26: *Omitto quod Varro dicit, omnes ab eis mortuos existimari manes deos.* The rest of the passage is ultimately from Servius, *Aen.* iii.63:

MANES. Manes sunt animae illo tempore, quo de aliis recedentes corporibus necdum in alia transierunt. Sunt autem noxiae, et dicuntur κατ' ἀντίφρασιν: nam manum, ut supra diximus, bonum est, unde et mane dictum est. similiter etiam Eumenidas dicimus, Parcas, bellum, lucum. alii manes a manando dictum intellegunt: nam animabus plena sunt loca inter lunarem et terrenum circulum, unde et defluunt. Quidam manes deos infernos tradunt. . . . alii manes nocturnos esse eius spatii, quod inter caelum terramque est, et ideo umoris qui noctu cadit potestatem habere: unde mane quoque ab isdem manibus dictum.

The borrowing is probably not direct; the extensive reordering of and additions to the passage, and the citing of Apuleius rather than Servius as the source of the information (cf. Arevalo's note on the section) point to an intermediate source, probably one of the numerous Vergilian scholiasts who drew upon Servius. The last etymology cited by Isidore is the correct one. *Manus* was Old Latin for *bonus;* and the dead, like fairies (the "Good People") and other supernatural beings were commonly called by euphemistic names in an attempt to ward off their malign influences.

101. *Larvas ex hominibus factos daemones aiunt, qui meriti mali fuerint. Quarum natura esse dicitur terrere parvulos et in angulis garrire tenebrosis.*

This section is an amalgamation of Augustine, *De civ. Dei* ix.11 (*dicit quidem et animas hominum daemones esse et ex hominibus fieri Lares si boni meriti sunt; Lemures, si mali, seu Larvas*) and Jerome, *Hebr. Quaes. in Gen.,* Praefatio (*quarum natura esse dicitur terrere parvulos et in angulis garrire tenebrosis*). It is odd that Isidore should omit the Lares from his discussion of *manes* and *larvae.* Whether there is any truth to the theory that the *Lares* were originally the beneficent ghosts of virtuous men is uncertain, but there may be some connection between the words *lar* and *larva* (see Dessau, *PW,* "Lares").

102. *Lamias, quas fabulae tradunt infantes corripere ac laniare solitas, a laniando specialiter dictas.*

I do not know where Isidore found his information on *lamiae;* perhaps it goes back to Varro, though the extant text makes no mention of them. Of course, the name has nothing to do with *laniare.* The lamia was originally a Greek rather than a Roman superstition, and her name is likewise Greek, though related etymologically to Latin *lemur;* it means something like "devourer." The tradition that she (or they) stole and devoured children is to be found in Horace, *Ars poet.* 340, in which the poet mentions the folk tale motif of the child swallowed alive and later cut from the lamia's maw, like Red Ridinghood from the wolf. Like many true folk superstitions, that of the lamia survived in Greece and the Balkans until modern times (Schwenn, *PW,* "Lamia").

103. *Pilosi, qui Graece Panitae, Latine Incubi appellantur, sive Inui ab ineundo passim cum animalibus. Unde et Incubi dicuntur ab incumbendo, hoc est stuprando. Saepe enim inprobi existunt etiam mulieribus, et earum peragunt concubitum: quos daemones Galli Dusios vocant, quia adsidue hanc peragunt inmunditiam.*

Pilosi . . . appellantur is from Gregory the Great, *Moralia* vii.15 (*Qui namque alii pilosi appellatione figurantur, nisi hi quos Graeci Panas, Latini incubos vocant?*) Isidore has changed *Panes* to *Panitae* (which Arevalo says should read *Panisci*); he may have been using a variant text. *Appellantur* appears to be introduced from Servius, *Aen.* vi.775, whence also *Inui . . . dicuntur* (*Inuus autem Latine appellatur, Graece* Πάν: *item* 'Επιάλτης *Graece, Latine Incubo: idem Faunus, idem Fatuus, Fatuculus. Dicitur autem Inuus ab ineundo passim cum omnibus animalibus, unde et Incubo dicitur); ab incumbendo, hoc est stuprando* may be Isidore's addition. The remainder of the section is from Augustine, *De civ. Dei* xv.23:

Et quoniam creberrima fama est, multique se expertos vel ab eis qui experti essent, de quorum fide dubitandum non esset, audisse confirmant, Silvanos et Panes, quos vulgo incubos vocant, inprobos saepe extitisse mulieribus et earum appetisse ac peregisse concubitum, et quosdam daemones, quos Dusios Galli nuncupant, adsidue hanc inmunditiam et temptare et efficere plures et tales adseverant ut hoc negare inpudentiae videatur, . . .

The *pilosi* are simply the "shaggy ones," an apt epithet for satyrs as they are commonly conceived. *Incubus* is from *incubo*, not *incumbo*, though the meanings of the two verbs are much the same (Kroll, *PW*, "Incubo"). He was thought to be a goblin who sent erotic dreams or nightmares; because of his lascivious nature, he was associated with Faunus and Pan. Inuus, according to Otto (*PW*, "Faunus"), takes his name not from *ineo* but from *in-avos*, "friendly," "beneficial," (cf. *aveo* and Greek ἰυής) and was either identical with the fructifying god

Faunus or a similar deity. *Dusius* comes probably from a Celtic root (perhaps it is related to Scand. *Tusse*, "fairy"). Isidore appears to be trying to derive it from *adsidue*, which is not justified by Augustine's use of the adverb.

104. *Quem autem vulgo Incubonem vocant, hunc Romani Faunum ficarium dicunt. Ad quem Horatius dicit (C. 3,18,1):*

> *Faune, Nympharum fugientium amator,*
> *per meos fines et aprica rura*
> *lenis incedas.*

Quem autem . . . dicunt is from Jerome, *Comm. in Isaiam* 13:21–22: *Pilosi saltabunt ibi; vel incubones, vel satyros, vel silvestres quosdam homines, quos nonnulli fatuos ficarios vocant, . . .* Many editors have changed Jerome's *fatuos* to *faunos* on the strength of Isidore's readings in this section and in *Origines* xi.3.22 (*quos nonnulli Faunos ficarios vocant*). It may be that Isidore had a variant text of Jerome; *faunus* and *fatuus* were used interchangeably (cf. Macrobius on the feminine version *Fatua/Fauna*, *Sat.* i.12.21). Otto (*PW*, "Faunus") see a connection between the adjective *ficarius* applied to Faunus and the fructifying nature of the fig; Frazer (commentary to Ovid's *Fasti*, Vol. II, pp. 344ff.) speculates that the women who conducted sacrifices to Juno Caprotina used twigs and sap from the male fig tree in a ritual intended to fertilize not only the female fig tree but also themselves. The quotation from Horace is unlikely to be direct, since Isidore gives the poet's name.

BIBLIOGRAPHY

1. Abbreviations of standard reference works and collections used in the text and bibliography.

CAH   *Cambridge Ancient History.* Cambridge: University Press, 1970–71.
CCSL   Corpus Christianorum, Series Latina.
CSEL   Corpus Scriptorum Ecclesiasticorum Latinorum.
HGM   Rose, H. J. *A Handbook of Greek Mythology.* New York: E. P. Dutton & Co., Inc., 1959.
OCD   *Oxford Classical Dictionary.* 2nd ed. Oxford: Clarendon Press, 1970.
PL   Migne, J.-P. (ed.) Patrologia Latina.
PW   *Paulys Realencyclopaedie der Classischen Altertumswissenschaft.* Edited by G. Wissowa *et al.* Stuttgart: Alfred Druckenmüller, 1893–1974.
TLL   *Thesaurus Linguae Latinae.* Leipzig: Teubner, 1900–1966.

2. Texts of Isidore of Seville, *Origines sive Etymologiae.*

Arevalo, Faustino (ed.) *S. Isidori Etymologiarum libri XX.* (PL, Vol. LXXXII.) Paris: Garnier Fratres, 1878.
Lindsay, W. M. (ed.) *Isidori Hispalensis Episcopi Etymologiarum sive Originum Libri XX.* 2 vols. Oxford Classical Texts. Oxford: Clarendon Press, 1911.

3. Texts of other authors.

Apuleius. *Opera Quae Supersunt.* Vol. III: *De Philosophia Libri: Liber de Deo Socratis, Liber de Mundo.* Edited by Paul Thomas. Leipzig: Teubner, 1938.
Arnobius. *Adversus Nationes.* Edited by A. Reifferscheid. (CSEL, Vol. IV.) Vienna: C. Geroldi Filius, 1875.
——. *Adversus Gentes.* (PL, Vol. V.) Paris: 1844.
Augustine. *De Baptismo contra Donatistas.* (PL, Vol. XLIII.) Paris: 1841.
——. *De Civitate Dei.* Edited by E. Hoffmann. 2 vols. (CSEL, Vol. XL.) Vienna: F. Tempsky, 1899.
——. *De Consensu Evangelistarum.* Edited by F. Weihrich (CSEL, Vol. XLIII.) Vienna: F. Tempsky, 1904.
——. *Contra Faustum Manichaeum.* (PL, Vol. XLII.) Paris: 1841.
——. *De Genesi ad Litteram.* (PL, Vol. XXXIV.) Paris: 1841.
——. *Contra Secundinum Manichaeum.* (PL, Vol. XLII.) Paris: 1841.
——. *Sermones.* (PL, Vol. XXXVIII.) Paris: 1841.
——. *De Trinitate.* (PL, Vol. XLII.) Paris: 1841.
Cassiodorus. *Expositio Psalmorum.* (CCSL, Vols. XCVII–XCVIII.) Turnhout: Brepols, 1958.

Catullus. *Carmina.* Edited by E. T. Merrill. Cambridge, Massachusetts: Harvard University Press, 1893.
Cicero. *De Re Publica, De Legibus.* Edited with an English translation by C. W. Keyes. Loeb Classical Library. Cambridge, Massachusetts: Harvard University Press, 1951.
——. *De Natura Deorum.* Edited by W. Ax. Stuttgart: Teubner, 1968.
Cyprian. *De Idolorum Vanitate (Quod Idola Non Dii Sunt).* (PL, Vol. IV.) Paris: 1841.
Donatus. *Commentarium Terenti.* Edited by Paul Wessner. 2 vols. Leipzig: Teubner, 1902.
Eucherius. *Instructiones.* (CSEL, Vol. XXXI.) Vienna: F. Tempsky, 1894.
Eusebius. *Chronici Canones: Latine Vertit, Adauxit, ad Sua Tempora Produxit S. Eusebius Hieronymus.* Edited by J. K. Fotheringham. London: Humphrey Milford, 1923.
Filastrius. *Diversarum Hereseon Liber.* Edited by F. Marx. (CSEL, Vol. XXXVIII.) Vienna: F. Tempsky, 1898.
Fulgentius. *Opera: Mitologiae.* Edited by Rudolf Helm. Stuttgart: Teubner, 1970.
Galen. *Opera Omnia.* Vol. IV: *De Usu Partium Corporis Humani* xvi, *De Semine* i. Edited by C. G. Kühn. Hildesheim: Georg Olms, 1964.
Gregory the Great. *Moralia.* (PL, Vol. LXXVI.) Paris: 1857.
Horace. *Odes and Epodes.* Edited by Paul Shorey and G. J. Laing. The Students' Series of Latin Classics. Chicago, New York, and Boston: Benj. H. Sanborn & Co., 1919.
Hyginus. *Astronomica.* Edited by E. Chatelain and P. Legendre. Paris: Librairie Honoré Champion, 1909.
——. *Fabulae.* Edited by H. J. Rose. Leyden: A. W. Sijthoff, n.d.
Jerome. *Commentarium in Ecclesiasten.* Edited by D. Johannes Martianaeus. (PL, Vol. XXV.) Paris: 1865.
——. *Commentarium in Epistolam ad Ephesios.* Edited by D. Johannes Martianaeus. (PL, Vol. XXVI.) Paris: 1866.
——. *Commentaria in Epistolam ad Titum.* Edited by D. Johannes Martianaeus. (PL, Vol. XXVI.) Paris: 1866.
——. *Commentaria in Ezechielem.* (CCSL, Vol. LXXV.) Turnhout: Brepols, 1964.
——. *Commentaria in Isaiam.* (PL, Vol. XXIV.) Paris: 1865.
——. *Commentaria in Isaiam.* (CCSL, Vol. LXXIII.) Turnhout: Brepols, 1969.
——. *Commentaria in Mattheum.* (PL, Vol. XXVI.) Paris: 1866.
——. *Commentaria in Mattheum.* (CCSL, Vol. LXXVII.) Turnhout: Brepols, 1969.
——. *Commentaria in Prophetas Minores.* (CCSL, Vol. LXXVI.) Turnhout: Brepols, 1969.
——. *Epistolae.* Edited by D. Johannes Martianaeus. (PL, Vol. XXII.) Paris: 1877.
——. *Liber Hebraicarum Quaestionum in Genesim.* (PL, Vol. XXIII.) Paris: 1865.
——. *Liber de Nominibus Hebraicis.* Edited by D. Johannes Martianaeus. (PL, Vol. XXIII.) Paris: 1865.
——. *Liber de Nominibus Hebraicis.* (CCSL, Vol. LXXII.) Turnhout: Brepols, 1959.
——. *Liber de Situ et Nominibus Locorum Hebraicorum.* Ed. D. Johannes Martianaeus. (PL, Vol. XXIII.) Paris: 1865.
——. *Vita S. Pauli Primi Eremitae.* Edited by D. Johannes Martianaeus. (PL, Vol. XXIII.) Paris: 1865.
Junius Philargyrius. *Explanatio in Vergilii Bucolica.* Edited by G. Thilo. In Servius, *Commentarii in Virgili Carmina,* edited by G. Thilo and H. Hagen, Vol. III. Leipzig: Teubner, 1887.
Lactantius. *De Ira Dei.* Edited by S. Brandt and G. Laubmann. (CSEL, Vol. XXVII.) Vienna: F. Tempsky, 1893.
——. *De Opificio Dei.* Edited by S. Brandt and G. Laubmann. (CSEL, Vol. XXVII.) Vienna: F. Tempsky, 1893.

——. *Institutiones Divinae.* Edited by S. Brandt and G. Laubmann. (CSEL, Vol. XIX.) Vienna: F. Tempsky, 1890.
Leander. *Regula, Homilia in Laudem Ecclesiae.* (PL, Vol. LXXII.) Paris: 1849.
Macrobius, *Saturnalia.* Edited by J. Willis. 2 vols. Leipzig: Teubner, 1963.
Ovid. *Fasti.* Edited with an English translation by J. G. Frazer. Loeb Classical Library. Cambridge, Massachusetts: Harvard University Press, 1967.
——. *Metamorphoses.* Edited with an English translation by F. J. Miller. 2 vols. Loeb Classical Library. Cambridge, Massachusetts: Harvard University Press, 1966.
Plato. *Laws.* Edited with an English translation by R. C. Bury. 2 vols. Loeb Classical Library. Cambridge, Massachusetts: Harvard University Press, 1926.
Prudentius. Edited with an English translation by H. J. Thomson. 2 vols. Loeb Classical Library. Cambridge, Massachusetts: Harvard University Press, 1949.
Quintilian. *Institutio Oratoriae.* Edited by L. Radermacher and V. Buchheit. Leipzig: Teubner, 1959.
Servius. *Commentarii in Vergilii Carmina.* Edited by G. Thilo and H. Hagen. 3 vols. Leipzig: Teubner, 1887.
Solinus. *Collectanea Rerum Memorabilium.* Edited by T. Mommsen. Berlin: Weidmann, 1895.
Tertullian. *Apologeticus Adversus Gentes.* (PL, Vol. I.) Paris: 1844.
——. *De Carne Christi.* (PL, Vol. II.) Paris: 1844.
——. *Ad Nationes.* (PL, Vol. I.) Paris: 1844.
——. *Quae Supersunt Omnia.* Edited by F. Oehler. 3 vols. Leipzig: T. O. Weigel, 1851–54.
——. *De Spectaculis.* (PL, Vol. I.) Paris: 1844.
Varro. *De Lingua Latina.* Edited with an English translation by Roland G. Kent. 2 vols. Loeb Classical Library. Cambridge, Massachusetts: Harvard University Press, 1938.
Vatican Mythographers. *Scriptores Rerum Mythicarum Latini Tres Romae Nuper Reperti.* Edited by G. H. Bode. Hildesheim: Georg Olms, 1968.
Vergil. *Aeneid.* Edited by T. E. Page. 2 vols. Classical Series. New York: St. Martin's Press, 1967.
——. *Bucolica et Georgica.* Edited by T. E. Page. Classical Series. St. Martin's Press, 1972.

4. Authorities.

ALLEN, W. S. "Ancient Ideas on the Origin and Development of Language," *Trans. Philolog. Soc.* (1948), pp. 35–60.
BEESON, CHARLES HENRY. *Isidor-Studien.* ("Quellen und Untersuchungen zur lateinischen Philologie des Mittelalters," 4, No. 2) Munich: C. H. Beck'sche, 1913.
BREHAUT, ERNEST. *An Encyclopedist of the Dark Ages: Isidore of Seville.* ("Studies in History, Economics and Public Law," 48 No. 1.) New York: Columbia University, 1912.
CURTIUS, ERNST ROBERT. *European Literature and the Latin Middle Ages.* Translated by Willard R. Trask. ("Bollingen Series," 36.) New York: Pantheon Books, 1953.
DRESSEL, E. "De Isidori Originum Fontibus," *Rivista di Filologia e di Instruzione Classica,* 3 (1875): pp. 207–268.
EBERT, ADOLF. *Allgemeine Geschichte der Literatur des Mittelalters in Abendland.* 2 vols. Leipzig: F. C. Vogel, 1889.
FONTAINE, JACQUES. *Isidore de Seville et la Culture Classique dans l'Espagne Wisigothique.* 2 vols. Paris: Etudes Augustiennes, 1959.
FOWLER, W. WARDE. *Roman Festivals of the Period of the Republic.* London: Macmillan, 1899.
FRAZER, SIR JAMES G. (ed.) *The Fasti of Ovid: Edited with a Translation and Commentary.* 5 vols. London: Macmillan and Co., Ltd., 1929.
HARDEN, D. B. "The Topography of Punic Carthage," *Greece and Rome* 9 (1939): pp. 1–12.

LAISTNER, M. L. W. "The Christian Attitude to Pagan Litera-ture," *History* 20 (1935): pp. 49–54.

——. *Christianity and Pagan Culture in the Later Roman Empire*. Ithaca, New York: Cornell University Press, 1951.

LINDSAY, W. M. "The Editing of Isidore's *Etymologiae*," *Classical Quarterly* 5 (1911): pp. 42–53.

PASCAL, PAUL. "Medieval Uses of Antiquity," *Classical Journal* 61 (1966): pp. 193–197.

PHILIPP, HANS. *Die historisch-geographischen Quellen in den etymologiae des Isidorus von Sevilla*. (Quellen und Forsch-ungen zur alten Geschichte und Geographie," Vol. XXVI, No. 2.) Berlin: Weidmannsche, 1913.

PURSER, L. C. Review of Lindsay's edition of the *Origines*, *Hermathena* 36 (1912): p. 188.

RAND, E. K., "Is Donatus' Commentary on Virgil Lost?" *Classical Quarterly* 10 (1916): pp. 158–164.

ROSE, H. J. *Ancient Roman Religion*. ("Hutchinson's Uni-versity Library. World Religions," No. 27.) London: Hutchinson's University Library, 1948.

SANDYS, J. E. "A Correction of Isidore, VIII.xi §83," *Classical Review* (1915), pp. 139–140.

SHARPE, WILLIAM D. "Isidore of Seville: The Medical Writings." *Trans. Amer. Philos. Soc.*, New Series 54, Pt. 2. Philadelphia: 1964.

SANFORD, EVA MATTHEWS. "Famous Latin Encyclopedias," *Classical Journal* 44 (1948–1949): pp. 462–467.

INDEX I

GODS AND OTHER MYTHOLOGICAL OR SUPERNATURAL FIGURES

Numbers designated p. or pp. refer to pages in the Introduction (pp. 3–11).   Numbers designated § or §§ refer to sections in the text and commentary (pp. 11–36).

INDEX II

CLASSICAL AND PATRISTIC AUTHORS

Numbers designated p. or pp. refer to pages in the Introduction (pp. 3–11). Numbers designated § or §§ refer to sections in the text and commentary (pp. 11–36).

De consensu Evangelistarum: p. 7; §§1, 30.
Contra Faustum Manichaeum: p. 7; §§5, 17, 41, 51, 80, 92.
De Genesi ad Litteram: p. 7; §§1, 30.
Contra Secundinum Manichaeum: §18.
De Trinitate: p. 7; §11.

Cassiodorus: §14.
Catullus: §57.
Celsus: p. 4.
Cicero: pp. 5, 10; §1.
  De natura deorum: §§1, 30, 31, 34, 42, 53, 57, 61.
Columela: §68.
Cyprian: p. 7; §1.

Diodorus Siculus: §33.
Diogenes of Apollonia: §77.
Dionysius of Halicarnassus: §68.
Donatus: pp. 8; §§57, 82, 83, 93.

Eucherius: p. 8, 9; §§13, 18, 19, 23, 24, 26.
Eusebius: pp. 6, 7; §§9, 10, 43, 74.

Festus: p. 8; §§42, 43, 45.
Filastrius: §14.
Fulgentius: §39.

Galen: §76.
Gregory the Great: p. 7; §§27, 28, 103.

Hesiod: §§40, 76, 80.
Herodotus: §50.
Homer: §40.
Homeric Hymns: §§47, 72.
Horace: p. 9; §102.
  Carmina: §§35, 44, 57, 104.
Hyginus: §§47, 54, 55, 84.

Isidore (other than *Origines* viii.11): pp. 4, 6; §§29, 41, 50, 51, 54, 55, 59, 61, 71, 72, 77, 84.

Jerome: p. 9; §13.
  Commentaria in Ecclesiasten: p. 7; §26.
  Commentarium in Epistolam ad Ephesios: p. 7; §§18, 27.
  Commentaria in Epistolam ad Titum: §18.
  Commentaria in Ezechielem: p. 7; §23.
  Commentaria in Isaiam: p. 7; §§23, 33, 104.
  Commentaria in Mattheum: p. 7; §§19, 26.
  Commentaria in Prophetas Minores (Osee): p. 7; §24.
  Epistolae: p. 7; §§20, 21, 22.
  Liber Hebraicarum quaestionum in Genesim: p. 7; §7.
  Liber de nominibus Hebraicis: p. 7; §§6, 7, 18, 19, 23.
  Liber de situ et nominibus locorum Hebraicorum: p. 7; §§23, 24, 26.
Junius Philargyrius: pp. 7, 8; §§82, 83, 92, 96, 97.

Lactantius: p. 10.
  De ira Dei: p. 7; §1.
  De opificio Dei: §77.
  Institutiones Divinae: pp. 7, 9; §§1, 2, 3, 4, 6, 7, 8, 15, 17, 18, 20, 21, 25, 29, 30, 31, 32, 33, 34, 35, 36, 42, 47, 49, 53, 67, 68, 69, 70, 77, 84, 86, 92, 93, 94.
  (Epitome): p. 7; §95.
Leander: pp. 3.
Livy: §48.

Macrobius: §§42, 54, 55, 66, 77, 84, 87, 104.
Minucius Felix: §33.

Ovid: p. 9.
  Fasti: §§47, 52, 59, 61, 68, 76, 84, 104.
  Metamorphoses: §§35, 47, 52, 54, 55, 84.

Petronius: p. 4.
Plato: p. 4; §50.
Pliny the Elder: p. 4.
Plutarch: §68.
Prudentius: p. 7; §58.

Quintilian: pp. 5; §§38, 42.

Sallust: §50.
Servius: pp. 8, 10, 11.
  Aeneid: pp. 5, 7, 8, 9; §§3, 23, 30, 34, 37, 39, 40, 41, 43, 44, 45, 46, 47, 48, 49, 51, 52, 53, 54, 55, 57, 58, 60, 61, 62, 63, 64, 65, 67, 69, 73, 74, 76, 77, 78, 80, 81, 83, 84, 87, 88, 90, 93, 97, 99, 100, 103.
  Eclogues: p. 7; §§25, 72, 81, 82, 83, 94.
  Georgics: p. 7; §§25, 32, 43, 59, 69, 75, 79, 87.
Solinus: p. 7; §§74, 86.
Statius: §60.
Suetonius: p. 4.

Tacitus: §63.
Tertullian
  Apologeticus adversus gentes: §§1, 33.
  De idololatria: p. 7; §§11, 12, 13, 14, 37.
  Ad nationes: p. 7; §§1, 30, 36.
  De praescriptione haereticorum: p. 7; §22.

Varro: pp. 4, 5, 8, 10; §§3, 6, 30, 31, 32, 38, 43, 44, 45, 56, 57, 59, 60, 61, 62, 63, 65, 66, 76, 77, 81, 84, 85, 88, 90, 95, 99, 100, 102.
  De lingua latina: pp. 4, 5, 8; §§30, 34, 38, 39, 42, 50, 53, 56, 57, 69, 84, 87, 90, 94, 96.
Vatican Mythographers: §§54, 55, 80, 81.
Vendicianus Afer: §77.
Vergil: pp. 7, 8, 9, 11.
  Aeneid: §§35, 42, 52, 57, 60, 69, 87, 95.
  Eclogues: §81.
  Georgics: §§70, 78, 81.
Verrius Flaccus: pp. 4, 8.

www.ingramcontent.com/pod-product-compliance
Lightning Source LLC
Chambersburg PA
CBHW050350110426
42812CB00008B/2426